tattoo on the heart

Paul J. Dabdoub

San Diego, CA, USA

S

Printed in the United States of America.

**INTERACT WITH PAUL
& OTHER READERS AT:**

www.TATTOOontheHEART.com

ACKNOWLEDGEMENTS

My beautiful wife, Mochacita and daughters Victoria & Jadyn – the laughs, struggles, and love we've shared have made me know God's love more than anything could.

In No Particular Order:

Mom, Dad, Maynard, Desi, Lorrie, Nanny, Pawpaw, the rest of the fam., Adrian, Bobby & Anna, Nick, Tom, Lon, AJ & Della, Lee & Marie, Phil, Brian, Crispin, Peter, Joe & Pat, Pete, Seth, Matt, Nikki, Stephanie, & Everybody @ EPIC Orlando, Ammar, Sean & Everybody @ EPIC San Diego, Chris H., Ben Comer, Susan, Jay Davis, Ben & Mark Langevin, Jon, Chris & Jan, Duke & Marie

+ all my students in 3 states that have challenged me & allowed me the chance to share in their lives. You mean the world to me & you've inspired me!

MY CONFESSION

I figured out God a long time ago.

I don't know exactly when it happened. I know I attended church some 300 times while I was still suspended in amniotic fluid.

Maybe it was when I was 4 at my home in Dyersburg, Tennessee doing my best imitation of a Southern preacher. At the conclusion of every message – on hell, mind you – my sister accepted Christ, whether she was willing or not. And none of the family could leave the living room until they shook my hand telling me what a great job I'd done.

Maybe it was immediately following my baptism. I walked with great difficulty to the back dressing room to shed my waterlogged 20 lb pair of Toughskin jeans. I was a walking wet floor hazard, and, to demonstrate, I slipped and landed on the back of my head a trinity of times.

I'm not sure when I figured God out, but I did.

I can't take all the credit for it. In 3rd grade, I left that evil, corrupting influence of the world – public schools – for the safe, pristine, virgin world of Christian school. Chapel services, creation-based science, and Scripture memorization helped me become a God-know-it-all.

MY CONFESSION

Something happened though.

Somewhere between puberty, seeing the moral failures of Christian leaders who were close to me, having my life run by legalistic, judgmental church people, and failing at my own attempts to earn salvation by grace through faith, I decided I just couldn't do this anymore.

By the time I was 19 years old, I effectively walked away from church. I wasn't done with God so to speak; I was just tired of being such a failure. I'd never please Him. I was tired of faking it. Even though victorious has been a way some people have described Christians, I spent most of my life feeling defeated. I honestly wasn't that different than people who didn't believe in Jesus. I wasn't that changed internally. I was racked with guilt. I tried so hard, did good for a while, then the wheels would fall off again.

I was supposed to be different! Was I ever really changed? I seemed to have signed up for an endless to-do list from going to church, reading my Bible, to evangelism, and I couldn't even manage my sin long enough to hardly think about that stuff. And even when I did, you know, I just really didn't feel like doing it.

I'm pretty sure I'm not alone. In fact, I see that most of this emerging generation of Christians have done the same as I did. At the risk of failing or faking, they have walked away from church altogether. 80% of the kids who grew up in church are done with it by the time they take their first ACT test.

We all have our stories. It doesn't matter if you grew up Catholic, Baptist, Pentecostal, Church of Christ, Presbyterian, etc., all of us – even those who never technically walked way from church, even those who had a healthy relationship *with* church – have carried on our lives with a dysfunctional relationship with God.

Just so we're clear: I'm not church or denomination bashing. Let's settle that right now. Beautiful, well-intentioned,

tattoo on the heart

God-fearing Christians spoke what they believed was God's Word to me to help me grow, mature, and to keep me from having sex before I got married. I thank them.

But I confess that I effectively walked away from it all because, though I knew every Scripture about Him, was well versed in theology, won Bible drills (if you don't know what they are, you're better off!), and had all the traditional markings of a healthy Christian, I was dying inside.

I thought I knew God. I figured Him out a long time ago. But I was wrong. I was so wrong. And my incomplete, inaccurate picture of Him kept me from the fullest life of gratitude, grace, joy, triumph, love, compassion, passion, humility, fun, community, friendship, meaning, breathing, smiling, giving, just to name a few.

Regardless of where you are living right now, God has given me a passion and a burden for you.

Struggling, defeated, ready to give up?

Hurt, bitter, angry because of what church did to you?

Pretty sure you've already made your mind up about what Jesus is all about?

Trying to figure out why you've got your life together and no one else does? Okay, that was sarcastic.

Let's chat awhile.

CONTENTS

01

tattoo of the heart

THE other day someone told me they thought the Flint-stones were making a comeback. No one I know is on the edge of their seat watching Flintstone fansites, but when your last name is pronounced "Dab-doo," and Fred has eas-ily become a large chunk of your persona and family heritage, it's good news.

At nearly 21 years of age, I succumbed to the reality that Fred and I would never be separated from one another. Like Waco and Koresh, Ozzy and bats, Bobby Knight and chairs, time may pass, I might do other things, accomplish something notable, get a reality TV show, but at the end of the day, the only thing that anyone will ever remember is that my ancestors were a prophetic cult following of the first animated primetime TV series modeled after the Hon-eymooners.

I really gave in to the affinity with Fred in a big way. It's funny because as a child I told people who made the com-parison between us to shut-up. It amazed me in high

1

school when really creative, insightful people would come up to me and say:

"Paul Dabdoub. Yabba Dabba Do! Has anyone ever said that to you?"

Incredulously, and with a sincere tone I'd reply: "No, you're the first one. Did you come up with that all by yourself?"

When I gave in, I gave in deep – about 7 or 8 layers deep. I stood in line behind 20 various military personnel who were getting tattoos with tough, manly things like swords, skulls, credos, their wife's name, and I walked up to my tattoo artist with a picture of Fred Flintstone with his hands raised that I'd found in a checkbook ad.

About 30 minutes later, my new ink sealed my connection with Fred for the rest of my lifetime.

I was pretty happy walking out of Beale Street Tattoos in Memphis, but it didn't take long before I started hearing criticism:

"Paul, you're going to be an old man in a nursing home one day, and people are going to see that tattoo and make fun of you."

 "That tattoo might keep you from getting a job." After all, this was still the South.

The more difficult thing was going back to my church basketball league. I wasn't attending church at the time and played basketball incognito. The tattoo was on my ankle, so I just kept my socks pulled up 80's style. Then one day it happened – my sock pulled down slightly to reveal Fred's left hand. Someone noticed - because church people have that kind of radar. By the look on their faces, you'd have thought it was the mark of the beast. I was caught. I'm ashamed to say that at legal drinking age, I almost told these people that it was a wash-off.

I should have known. I was really familiar with the aura of those tattooed people who came to our church when I was growing up. They were in to something or they were carrying around the shame of their past. They couldn't be good Christians. They probably didn't even use their turn signal when they changed lanes.

I still had one more huge obstacle...

A week later, mom came to visit, and I showed off my new ink. She wasn't really keen on it because I'd committed what she considered an obvious Biblical transgression. In her usual direct way enhanced by an East Tennessee accent she reminded me:

"The Bible says not to tattoo your body."

And it does say that. Of course, within that same chapter of various laws in Leviticus 19, it says a number of other things as well:

> "Do not mate different kinds of animals."
> "Do not plant your field with two kinds of seed."
> "Do not wear clothing woven of two kinds of material."
> "Do not cut the hair at the sides of your head or clip off the edges of your beard."

It's pretty obvious that that we don't usually reference the majority of these kinds of laws. There are a few laws in this chapter that we do think are still valid like not forcing your daughter into prostitution. That's a good law I think.

But it's safe to say that it would be dangerous to impractical or mildly silly to practice a lot of these things today.

However, I don't want to give you the impression that there are things in the Bible that we just throw out or dismiss. They are still in there. And I think it's our duty to learn the why behind it. Historically, what was going on? Who was doing the speaking and who were they speaking to? What was the significance of the law?

When the Scripture says, "Do not put a stumbling block in front of the blind" is it safe to assume that there were a lot of practical jokers back in that day?

GOING BACK TO TATTOOS...

Let's take a closer look:

Some of the laws stated in this chapter were about morality (right and wrong), others were about health (not eating poorly cooked meat), and the rest were about differentiating themselves from pagans.

Here's where we usually stop.

In our modern day application of these verses, Christians seem to focus in like a laser beam on the set-apartness of God's people as a set of standards set on certain behaviors like voting preferences, appearance, and the removal from the whole of culture. It might mean your kids go to a Christian school, you have a fish swimming on the back of your car, or your radio is welded on a Christian station. In other words, we focus more on what is being done and the command to be different rather than the real "why" behind it all.

In this passage, do we really think that all God was concerned about was haircuts and outward expressions of religious allegiance? Did God just want people who were a little quirky and borderline obsessive-compulsive when compared to other peoples? Somehow, I think this is all a far cry from the set-apartness that God truly wanted.

God is speaking to His covenant people Israel. When He tells them not to do something, it's not because He didn't want them to be fashionable or trendy, nor did He want them to be counter-cultural. He is specifically telling them to stay far from the religious practices of the surrounding people groups. The prohibited religious practices in these verses included eating bloody meat, fortune telling, cutting or marking the body for dead relatives, cultic prostitution and consulting psychics. Even certain bad haircuts were a kind of "sacrifice of the hair" to false gods.

Tattooing was a common practice in that day. Often people would tattoo themselves with pictures and symbols of people who died as a part of a pagan mourning rite. Others would tattoo themselves showing their identification or allegiance to a particular diety.

You might remember a scene in the movie Gladiator when Maximus uses a sharp rock to cut his military tattoo off his arm. Juba, another gladiator slave, saw the tattoo and asked Maximus: "Is that the mark of your gods?"

It is important to note here that the context of this passage is not one of body décor but one of marking one's self in connection with cultic religious worship. With the Hebrew track record of idolatry throughout the entire Old Testament, it is safe to assume that they weren't merely part of a growing fad, they were willingly participating in pagan worship.

BUT THERE'S A MUCH DEEPER ISSUE...

The whole point is that what the Jews had been doing here was not a passive reflection of the surrounding culture. They were actively engaging in something vehemently opposed to God.

God really did want a people who were set apart – a holy people who differentiated themselves from the whole of humanity. We identify ourselves with that as Christians today. Unfortunately, for most of our recent existence as the Church, we've spent the majority of our time avoiding culture itself as though culture in and of itself is equated with the worship of false gods. We've opposed things, forbidden things, separated ourselves from things, all in the name of being different. But differentiating ourselves isn't the same thing as being holy and set apart to God.

SOMEHOW, WE MISSED THE POINT...

While there were a lot of forbidden practices for the Jews to separate themselves, there was also a "do" list – those things that were a sign that Jews followed the one, true God. The most definitive visual *mark* that a Jew could give would be that of circumcision.

Circumcision was instituted in the 12th and 15th chapters of Genesis when God made unconditional promises to Abraham that his descendants would be more numerous than the stars in the sky; that through his descendants all the nations would be blessed; and that Abraham's people would be given a great land to occupy and that all who blessed them would in turn be blessed.

The key here is that circumcision was to be a "sign of the covenant" that had already been given to Abraham with no strings attached. The point of circumcision was that it was supposed to be an outward symbol, a reminder of the relationship that God had with these people. It wasn't a symbol of what they could do to earn that relationship; it wasn't a symbol of what they could do to keep it; it was a symbol of grace. God was saying, "On My own name I'm making a promise to you. No matter what you do, no matter what happens, you will be Mine. It's not about how good you are, it's about *My* goodness."

The sad reality is that circumcision became less about grace – this undeserved, unearned favor with God – and more about a religious ritual of something to do to earn God's favor.

A truly devout Jew would typically be defined as a person who spent their lifetime avoiding forbidden things and maintaining commanded religious practices including circumcision. And they got really good at it as well. As a matter of fact, over the course of hundreds of years, the Jews seemed to have put all that pagan worship behind them completely. They were doing all the right things, saying the right things, and avoiding all the things that would have defiled them. And then Jesus steps onto the scene and gives them a little review:

Matthew 15:8-9

> These people honor me with their lips, but their hearts are far from me. Their worship is a farce, for they teach man-made ideas as commands from God.

Huh? Hundreds of years of cleaning up, ousting of false gods, rules, and record-keeping and this is the kind of review these people get? And the worst part is that Jesus wasn't even original when He said this. As a matter of fact, He was quoting Isaiah who gave the same review hundreds of years before.

And the religious elite (known as Pharisees) that Jesus was talking to were irate. "Didn't it matter? Didn't it matter, Jesus, that we did all these things that we were commanded to do? Didn't it matter that we avoided all these connections to all that was unsacred? We did everything we were asked to do! How dare You!"

And Jesus was like, "You guys just don't get it do you?"

You see, something was implied when those kinds of commands in Leviticus were written. It should have been understood and profoundly experienced as a daily reminder when they saw the visual *reminder* on their very being. Isaiah made it blatantly obvious to the people who were missing it.

The point was not rule-keeping.
The point was not religious practices.

The point was not living differently than everyone else.
The point was not living more moral.
The point was not wearing the sign of circumcision.

And the Pharisees were astounded and resentful. They
acted as if Jesus was changing the "rules." But He wasn't.
Jesus was harkening back. He was making a plea. If the
laws, if the cutting flesh, if Isaiah's rant were only whispers,
Jesus wanted to make it abundantly clear that the point is,
was always, will always be, the heart.

The Jews mistakenly thought following the rules would
earn God's favor, and they'd get Him off their backs. But
the conversation God was trying to have with the Jews was
that He didn't want them to follow out insincerity, but out
of the devotion of their hearts.

The Pharisees did all the things right and wore the mark of
circumcision as an arrogant sign of their own perfection,
superiority, and righteousness. But God was trying to
point out the inferiority of that kind of mark and promised
a work that only He could accomplish within them:

> **Deuteronomy 30:6**
>
> The LORD your God will circumcise your heart, and
> the heart of your seed, to love the LORD your God
> with all your heart, and with all your soul, that you
> may live.

God was going to do some cutting. He was going to leave a
permanent mark. He would tattoo their hearts.

Is this relevant for today? Does all this sound strikingly
similar to you? It does to me. It sounds a lot like what
we've come to know as Christianity. Somehow, Christians
have come to be known as people who don't *do* certain
things. More specifically, we're known as people who are
against things, but known very little by what we are *for*.
Christians have a to-do list, just like our spiritual forefa-

thers the Jews. We do things to get God off our backs, to appease Him, or to point to our own arrogant superiority, while the whole time God is saying:

"You have my love. You have my favor. Receive it, and live out of it."

I think the simple reason that most Christians live so defeated, so guilt-ridden, I think the simple reason that 80% of teenagers who grew up in church walk away from God before they reach Christian adulthood, I think the reason why, with all our knowledge, good works, and outward signs, we still live so unchanged and condemned is because we haven't truly experienced the basic essential in the whole of humanity, in the whole of the Gospel – God loves us.

It's become cliché. It has no punch or power. You know why? Because God's love is something that we have a head knowledge of, but never has the height, depth, length or width of this love ever been truly experienced by the heart.

With Abraham, God wanted to start right there with an outward symbol, a physical scar, an actual surgical process to say: "Just as this is being carved into your flesh, I want to carve into your very being My love." And what did we do with it? We turned that very sign into something we had to do to earn love.

What is the command that surpasses all? What is the command that is foundational to everything in the Kingdom of Heaven? Love God with all your heart, mind, and strength.

If we truly breathed the truth of God's love into the depths of our beings, then we would be people who respond with extraordinary love and devotion. And you know what? That's all God wants from us. If God gets our love, then everything else is just details.

OKAY, TELL ME SOMETHING
I DON'T KNOW...

I'm not pretending to say something that hasn't already been said. In fact, I'm sure I'm saying something that you already know. But when I say "know," understand that I mean with a head knowledge. We *know* it. We *believe* it.

But let me ask you this: Have you *experienced* it?

We do want to be people who love God. But that feels so far away, so distant. We seem so helpless to even begin to do such a thing, especially with our whole being.

I'm pretty confident that this "loving God with our whole hearts" can't take place until our hearts are made whole.

Loving God, giving Him what He desires – our very hearts – is a response.

Here's what Paul said about this to the church at Ephesus:

> I pray that out of His glorious riches He may strengthen you with power through His Spirit in your inner being, so that Christ may dwell in your hearts through faith. And I pray that you, being rooted and established in love, may have power, together with all the saints, to grasp how wide and long and high and deep is the love of Christ, and to know this love that surpasses knowledge—that you may be filled to the measure of all the fullness of God.

Paul's earnest desire for these Christians was that they would be rooted and grounded in the love of Jesus. "Rooted" is a botanical term that life is only given, sustained, and grown out of love. Like a plant can't survive without roots, we cannot survive unless our roots our firmly planted in love.

I think this is what Jesus intended in the Parable of the Soils. Jesus notes that some seed fell on rock. This wasn't plain rock, but slabs of limestone in certain parts of the field just under the surface with an inch or two of soil over them. The limestone would hold the warmth of the sun throughout the night, and for a while the new plants would spring up and grow vigorously, that is until they ran out of moisture. Since they couldn't get a root down into deep soil, they would quickly wither and die.

If we're defeated and dying, is what is rooting us something other than love. Do you know people who thrived and then faded into nothingness and defeat?

"Grounded" is an architectural term relating to foundation. A pastor friend of mine led a capital giving campaign for a new building on their existing church campus. A team of architects and consultants drew up plans for a state-of-the-art facility with what they felt was an adequate price tag. The church embraced the vision and gave, and one year later the construction began. The first week they began digging. At the end of the week they had to cut a heavy check for the work that was completed. The second week, more digging, and at the end of that week, another heavy check. This went on for weeks. It seemed no progress was being made besides digging and moving around dirt. My pastor friend was watching their bank account quickly emptying and was ever growing frustrated. He had no idea of how far the construction guys really had to dig to get a solid foundation. It cost a ton of money; more than they previously thought, because they made a lot of assumptions about the land. At any point they could have stopped digging and started building. If they didn't care about the longterm investment they were making, they could save money, build the structure, and eventually lose everything when it started falling apart. If they really didn't value life, they could have built a structure that could have functioned but at any moment could collapse and kill or severely injure people.

I wonder how many of us were building and creating structure long before we truly had a foundation. We're trying to do great things for God. Why? At the end of the day are we feeling weak, vulnerable, and questioning our status with God? Are we unfulfilled, ever seeking more? Is it possible that we are out building and building on a weak foundation? If it's not founded on love, we're going to implode. We just weren't made any other way.

The heart is powerful. It will run, it will go when our minds and bodies won't. But it's fragile. God found our hearts when we were completely broken. And for a lot of us, instead of allowing God to heal and make it whole, we went into performance mode. We quit sinning. We started looking and living differently. And now we're toast. Or at best, we're still plugging away, unhealthy, and feeling like frauds.

Can you take a moment to respond? Can you just put this book down along with all the stuff you have to *do* that seems so important, and make a move towards God that, if it doesn't just restore your life, it may very well *save* your life?

Paul's prayer was that these Christians would grasp (literally "seize") and know this love. "Know" here was the Greek word "ginosko" which meant a knowledge that was bigger than information. This knowledge was experiential.

How can you respond right now? Maybe you ask God right now to reveal to you the things that you've rooted yourself in. Ask God what you have used as your foundation that is not His love.

Move toward God, as best you know right now and ask Him:

"God, I want to seize your love. I want to know Your love. Lord, will You show me the depth, the height, the length, the width Your love is for me? Will you overwhelm me with the knowledge of Your love?"

Now what?

Keep praying that prayer. It's not a one time "yeah, I did that." We'll never know the fullness of His love, but God will continue to reveal it. He desires for you to know that love. As a matter of fact, our hitting walls, deflating circumstances, and breakdowns are all a part God's intentional design for us to find our being in, and only in, His love.

02

heart craving

THE MARRIAGE RETREAT

WE arrived at the Solomon Episcopal Retreat Center in
Robert, Louisiana about as early as we could possibly ar-
rive. The central building – where large group meetings
and hangout normally take place – contained the reception
area where you pick up your room keys, sign a waiver that
you won't trash your room, and get the short list of attrac-
tions around the multi-acre wooded campus.

While my wife Jessica talked to the hostess, I scanned the
room noticing a small contingency of married couples who
made nervous small talk around couches and tables that
marked off a common area. My attention was regained
when I heard the hostess mention there was free wine and
cheese over in the corner of the room. "Now that's the perk
of doing a marriage retreat at an Episcopal facility," I whis-
pered to my wife. My whispers are notoriously loud, and
Jessica's eyelids and facial muscles did a slight grip on her
eyeball momentarily signifying that I was being a little rude.

We got our keys and started walking toward the exit. A couple that we were pretty good friends with from the church nearly got mashed as I swung the door open. Despite the near miss, both were overjoyed to see us there and greeted us really warmly.

"We're going over to the table over there to play board games. Do you two want to join us?"

My wife and I - putting our oneness on display – said in conjunction: "Uh...No..." in a slightly exaggerated tone.

We took a brisk walk, putting it mildly, toward our room. I asked Jessica if she wanted me to run in and lift one of those bottles of wine. She said, "Maybe later, when not so many people are standing around."

We missed dinner and made it to the first session that night with just enough time to spare to fix a cup of coffee and walk in. A few people noticed us walking into the main meeting area and a woman said: "There you two are. You missed dinner. Did you have a difficult time finding the place?"

Jessica said, "What are you talking about we've been here all day. We've just been in our room the whole time." The woman responded with a less than pleasant "that's too much information for me" look on her face.

Like two school brats, we giggled as we found our seats.

The retreat leadership couple set up the entire weekend at the opening of the first session: "We don't want you guys to stay locked up in sessions with us all weekend. You're here to be with each other. We're going to discuss some things that maybe you've never talked about or that you haven't talked about in a long time. You'll spend some time with us in a large group format, but then I want you to go to a quiet place or back to your rooms (Jessica I looked at each other and high-fived) and spend some time together. We'll give you a couple of exercises to guide you, but they are only meant to help you connect."

The first session passed, we got our homework and went back to our rooms, talked, eliminated misconceptions we had about each other, laughed, wrestled out issues we'd never mentioned, made some commitments, made some future plans, and leaned in and savored our moment.

A couple of hours later, our stomachs reminded us that we'd forfeited our meal ticket blessing for a bowl of pottage, and that we needed to stop everything and scavenge for food. We trekked up to the common area to see if there was any cheese left and were shocked to find couples dotting the whole area.

Jessica looked at me and said, "What are all these people doing over here? Don't they know they have a room where they can hang out with each other....alone!"

On our way back to our room, we ran in to a couple on their first marriage retreat ever. They'd managed to leave a houseful of kids behind for the first time in 15 years. They hadn't been at our church long enough to meet most of the people who were attending the retreat, so we felt a little ob-ligated to hang out with them as we were walking back to our room. We finally arrived at that geographical cross-roads where if you keep walking you'll be going a different direction than where your room is.   I made that transition of "Our room is right down here." I watched the faces of this couple – particularly the man – morph to this "You're not going to leave us by ourselves are you?" look. He tried to tempt us with a game of Yahtzee – couple vs. couple no less! I, the consummate competitor, actually contemplated the challenge before my wife chimed in: "No, we're going to go hang out together tonight. We never get to be alone."

The rest of the weekend flowed in a similar vein. Every ses-sion presented some challenges that weren't designed to provide answers, but to point us in the direction where we'd discover them together, and, in the process, we'd discover each other. There weren't always simple fixes, but we walked out of there with the commitment to live, and breathe together as we determined to move toward each other after we left.

I wish I could say the same for every couple that was there that weekend. I painfully watched couples whose body language spoke anything but openness. In one session, we were all asked to take the next 15 minutes and lay hands upon and pray for our wives – aloud so that our wives could hear us. A few men refused. Others prayed in silence. Most couldn't pray for more than a minute or two.

It was in that moment that I saw marriages and home lives in context. I understood the board game people; I understood the people who didn't comprehend missing dinner; I understood competitive Yahtzee couple – they were all avoiding the same thing - namely intimacy. What would they do if they were just left by themselves? What would they talk about? What would come up?

These couples had never really known intimacy before this weekend. They were given the tools to make it happen. Some were unwilling. Some were apathetic. After all, intimacy is dangerous, reckless, and risky. If you peel back the layers of who you are, then it's possible for that person to say: "I don't like what I see, and I'm done with you." It's possible that if you're real and speak the truth the other may not be able to handle it. It's difficult to be weak and needy. It's so much easier to put up a front and act like you've got it together. It's humbling to say "You're right, and I'm wrong." It's not even human to prefer someone above yourself – even in the moment.

But what is marriage without intimacy? It's shallow. It's going through the motions. It's unfulfilling. It's not the dream that you pictured on wedding day. And it's more and more difficult to keep committing to that stinkin' ring every day.

Half of marriages fail – they end in divorce. The other half of marriages – they are fail*ing.* How many couples do you know that are in brutal, unhealthy marriages? How many couples are "committed to the marriage?" They will hold on to the commitment that they made to the marriage because it's just wrong to get a divorce. How many couples are "committed to the kids?"

I'm sorry but that's just not good enough. In fact, it sucks.

God doesn't want you to be committed to the relationship with Him. He doesn't want you to stay in this thing with Him because of a few good things that you've produced together. God won't settle for anything else but your whole heart. And the truth is, you're not willing to settle for anything else either!

INTIMACY IS NOT AN OPTION

I know if I ever get to a place where I'm just in a marriage with Jessica because of a document on paper, because of the tan line on my ring finger, or the commitment I made to her back in 2000 that my marriage is as good as dead.

Whenever Jessica and I have issues, things seem to get shaky, cross words are said, actions are misunderstood, the devil feeds us lies, or we are just not communicating, I can always trace it back to the loss of intimacy. Whenever things have precluded or taken the place of intimacy, dysfunction always ensues. We quickly become Yahtzee players - just being active - but hearts not connected. I struggle to put my hand on her forehead and scarcely know the words to pray.

Intimacy has to be fought for, battled for, and won. It is simply not an optional part of our marriage.

I find it's easy for Christians to get caught up in the things that take the place of intimacy with God: doing good, taking care of family, church activities, even spiritual disciplines. They all can give people the impression that everything is okay with ourselves and God. When inside, we know we couldn't be more distant than we are from Him.

I think we're well aware that things are missing. You can't fool your heart. We sense, we know "something is missing." We don't know "when we lost it," and we don't know how to get back there. In many cases, we can't find a thing that we've done to lose it, but we can open a file folder full of all the things that we've done to try to get it back. Most of these are religious duties sprinkled with empty spiritual hoops that haven't done a thing to bring us into an encounter with the living God.

We may not be able to put our finger on it enough to verbalize it, but our hearts definitely know something that our minds can't comprehend.

What is it? Our hearts are crying for intimacy with God. Our hearts are dying for a Person who will allow us to sincerely pull the layers back and love us for actually doing it. Our hearts want to be able to recklessly leap and be captured by Love. Is this a surprise for us? I mean our hearts were handcrafted this way by God.

Do you realize that what you truly desire is intimacy? I once tried to tell a teenager that and was met with the infamous "deer in headlights" look. No matter how true it is, the desire to know and experience and invisible God seems a little out there and far-fetched.

In the event that we take the suggestion of intimacy at face value, we take a wild shot in the dark at it, and it usually looks something like the guy struggling to pray for his wife – it's foreign, embarrassing, and ineffective. And like him, we ask the question: "Where do you even begin to do this thing?"

So since we're unable to make the intimacy with God thing happen, we go back to what we know - playing Yahtzee. "Let's get even busier and do things for God. Let's get involved in every church activity that we can. Let's join a ministry team." Shake the cup: read the Bible. It's activity – at least we're doing *something* – but it's far from intimacy.

If we never experience the depth of knowing God, if we never experience ongoing intimacy with Him, if we never get to pull the layers back and LIVE to tell about it, if we never risk and get to be loved by God, then our hearts will redirect toward other things – places where our heart is numbed - where at least the void of emptiness is filled.

So, how's your intimacy with God right now? Is it happening?

Your heart is in desperate need of repair. You need to be able to pull the layers back. You will never be fully alive until the layers are pulled back, your brokenness is revealed, and you find yourself still fully embraced by the Father.

Has it been a long time since you've been there, and now you're afraid of what might come up? Maybe you've never gone there. And there's a really good reason for that.

03

broken{heart}ed

As much as I've changed over the past several years in my thoughts about God, life, and the Bible, it still amazes me the number of things that I've never sat down and challenged and thought through. Take, for instance, Bible stories. Growing up in church, I heard every one about a million times. I would even correct the teacher from time to time.

So many of these same stories I still haven't revisited with my adult intellectual mind and my ever-expanding, yet more intimate & personal knowledge of God.

A few years back, I gave Adam and Eve a second look. Simplistic story right? Even people who've never have been to church somehow know this one. What's there to find?

You know what I find really sad about myself? You know a really good reason why I never look back at this story? I've been consumed a lot more with the fall than the intimate details that this story reveals.

21

At first glance, we hardly identify with these two people, except for the fact that they ultimately blow it and disappoint God. It's as though nothing was ever passed down from these people except a nature prone to brokenness and sin.

Let me ask you: Has this story ever tugged at your heart-strings?

So what is the story as you recall? Something like God speaks the world into existence over a period of 6 solid days capped off by creating man and taking a little nappy. Genesis is written chronologically, so it gives us the sense that God created Eve on Day 8 or so, then Day 9 or 10, they sin by eating from the Tree of Knowledge of Good and Evil, bringing the whole human race down with it.

I think that's a good outline of major events. But I think there's a lot of story and living that is right below the surface, if we can just go to this place that's seemed all too familiar and give it a fresh pair of eyes and heart.

So let's pick up with Day 8...

Man. He's perfect in every way and possesses authority & power – those are two really important things to guys. But somehow those things don't ultimately make him.

I mean, have you ever thought of Adam as a guy with dreams and ambition? I didn't used to think so. I thought he was bored. I always pictured him walking around a little garden all day eating fruit, or sitting on a rock with his hand under his chin as animals passed by him: "monkey...dog...lion...bear..." I don't know if you've noticed this, but animals in the wild don't just walk up to you to be named. If you have the picture of God creating a person who's the epitome of a spoiled, American teenager, then maybe Adam had Tivo, a stocked fridge within arm's reach, and even the menial tasks that he did have would be at his feet – or in this case walking right in front of him. C'mon!

Do you think this is a reflection of a perfect creation? Do you really think God just made lazy people with zero ambition?

Adam was an explorer. He climbed trees and mountains. He went on treks to the waters and dived down as far as he could, and for as long as he could, to experience life in the sea, encountering first hand and naming creatures. There was something about his life that was edgy, risky, and a sharpness that bit him everyday to make him want more.

He was fierce, tenacious, planning, dreaming, thinking outside the box, wondering what could be next. He had full authority & power from God – all he really needed to succeed. And he was succeeding. Things were being created from his hands. He was a traveler. The Garden was massive, not some 2 acre plot – it was a huge expanse. He was always seeing and experiencing, naming some millions of species. He'd seen and done a lot. But he was just so stinkin' lonely. Somehow all he did and accomplished at the end of the day missed some meaning. And God would watch him – God would have a smile on His face every day watching His mini-Him, dream, create, etc. But God also noticed the lack of his smile being full. And God had a plan for that too.

Let's say it took a hundred years for Adam to complete that first "little" job. He conquered in those years, but he noticed that no matter how close he got to those created things, no matter how much he accomplished, it was missing something. You know, if you've hung out with chimps for years and years, there's a gratitude and appreciation when a human being comes into existence.

Adam said, "This is now bone of my bones and flesh of my flesh..."

Doesn't sound that romantic, does it? But imagine everything that Adam was trying to put into words. You can't imagine how meaningful it must've been for Adam right there to have all of these things, to have accomplished so much, to have seen the world - it's beauty, it's danger - and now he's got someone to share that with. Not just anyone – someone who in many ways looks like him only more beautiful, more social, more relationally gifted, compassionate, emotional, contemplative – it was awesome. He felt so loved and embraced by God.

These weren't cut-out characters or coloring book people – but real human beings with hopes, dreams, emotions – doing life together. Man + Woman + God, and it was all perfect. I bet they didn't have self esteem issues. Adam? He admired and romanced her. Eve? She thought he was so brave, strong, and she was safe and secure. God? He's right in the center of it – walking with them. When they saw His face, they saw pleasure and love. And do you know what else they saw? They saw *themselves*.

Have you ever been to the hospital to see a family member who's just been born? When your family gathers at the window and looks into the incubator, what's the first thing they say? Right after the oooh's and ahhhh's, immediately family members start pointing out what features on the baby belong to them – "He's got my nose"..."He's got my eyes"..."No he doesn't! He's got my eyes." Family members will argue for years over who they think looks like whom. But what actually is going on? They are laying claim to that little baby as soon as they see him.

Parents do this all the time with their small children. I'm sure your parents did this a lot as well. "You look just me." Or, "You act just like your mom." They actually love those parts of you and can't help but pick you up and remind you of it constantly. You loved it, too. Boys want to be strong like dad. Girls put on their mom's high heel shoes and makeup if they can reach it. Your identity is taken from your parents.

It was the same way in the Garden of Eden. Adam and Eve had the perfect spiritual relationship with God, but they also had a physical relationship with Him.

What would it look like for a perfect loving Father to go on a walk with His kids? We know they walked with God in the garden. Perhaps that happened for years. I wonder what those conversations were like. I wonder if they walked hand-in-hand with God. I'm sure they did; those kids were everything to Him. God would win spin them around. Adam and Eve knew by the smile on His face that they were His pride and joy.

Just like your identity was wrapped up in your parents, Adam and Eve's was wrapped up in the image of God. When they looked at their Creator, they saw a resemblance to Him. And I think God even told them the same thing: "Adam, you remind me of Myself when you…and Eve, that smirk you get on your face, you got that from Me." How could Adam and Eve have not felt worth and acceptance when they looked at the Creator of the world and saw themselves?

In no way am I saying anything like: "We are gods," so don't go off on that tangent. I think in our brokenness, we struggle with the fact that we are made in God's image, and for Adam and Eve, that was everything. They were the only two humans on the planet. As far as living things go, their very likeness made them a minority; they were the only living things that looked like God. They were solid. They didn't have doubts. Doubts didn't enter their minds.

That's what is so heart-wrenching about this whole story. In the thousand times I heard or read this story, I was never emotional about it in the very least. It was because I couldn't identify with being perfect. I couldn't identify with being the creation of God. I couldn't identify with myself being made in the image of God. I mostly couldn't identify with God wanting to have a relationship like a real father with me.

25

I went to the park with my daughters yesterday. I would be devastated if that was the last time I would ever walk with them. I would hurt. I would grieve.

Well, you know what? God felt that way. God still feels that way. And our fears, our insecurities, our shame are all a direct result of the loss of that intimate relationship. It's been difficult for us not to see the smile of God's face as He looks at us. God being distant is not okay with us. We feel the need to be swung around in His arms and know the security that His love is never going away.

Adam's confidence, power, authority; Eve's safety, security – they were all wrapped up in relationship with God. The relationship was so strong, so pure that neither felt unclothed. They walked around so naked, they didn't even know they were naked. They weren't ignorant or innocent; they were just complete and unashamed. And when that relationship was broken, they knew it instantly because that clothing of security came from God. When it was gone, they were exposed. Insecurity arises the instant you know you are alone. Adam and Eve hid themselves. Their first emotions were fear, guilt, and shame.

Our identities never recovered from that. In his book, *Victory Over the Darkness*, Neil Anderson writes that what happened at the fall was a loss of the knowledge of God Himself that led to brokenness in our relationship with God, with others, and finally with ourselves. It might be difficult to grasp that the loss of knowledge of God could create such an identity crisis. But our identity was intrinsic to that relationship.

This is how lust originated. There is sexual lust, but sexual lust is not just lusting after another person's body. We're lusting after an intimate experience where we can be told that we are good, right, okay with the world, secure, and desired.

When movies portray sex, the common expression is "I want you." Teenage girls on talk shows who've had multiple sex partners at a young age talk about their desire to be "wanted" by guys. In courtroom scenes, we've been disgusted by sexual predators who would say that the person they raped or molested "wanted what they got." In all of these cases, it is the good desire of being wanted that has gone bad. The need is legitimate, and the brokenness in relationship has created a vacuum that is attempting to be filled.

Man who once had confidence, power, and authority bestowed by God now lusts for it. Because of the loss of relationship, the replacements became money, power, and status. We compare athleticism, beauty, checkbooks, sales contests, toys, and even more relational strife is born out of it.

We're usually in denial that Christians could be shallow people like this. Truth is, we find other ways to compare. Often we compare "blessings" that we've gotten from God. That's a way to spiritualize it. Or on the other side, we compare struggles with other people. Maybe that strikes a nerve with you.

You know what this is? It's brokenness with God. Our beliefs about God are wrong. Have you ever felt cheated – just a little by God? Maybe someone got something they didn't deserve. You might have struggled to be happy for one of your friends who just fell in love, won something, or got a promotion.

We often feel like life is this one pie, and when someone gets a big slice that there is less left for us. So we resent the person, because we resent God.

When our lives our difficult, we look at other people who seem to have fewer problems. Things are going their way, and they make us sick. Maybe we don't express it outwardly, but our hearts know all too well that we believe that

God loves them more, or He loves us less, or, at the very least, God is just not a good God.

It's all brokenness. Because of sin, our knowledge of God was lost which, in turn, caused us to even lose the knowledge of ourselves. Our perception of reality is twisted, and our identities are wrecked.

Ephesians 4:18

> They are darkened in their understanding and separated from the life of God because of the ignorance that is in them due to the hardening of their hearts.

Because of this lost knowledge of God, the epicenter of our hurt lies in our hearts, and that's where God wants to work in us. God's desire is to fully bring us back to life. The word life that's used in this passage is the word "zoe," which in a literal sense is the highest form of life that is made vital by Jesus Himself. It's the life that is brought about because we literally found it *in* Him.

If He can heal our hearts and we can truly know Him again, then our identities can be put back together. We can know who we are. We can know that we are already loved. We can feel secure again. Our passions will be back in balance. We won't waste our time comparing with other people. We won't be ashamed if we don't measure up in the world's eyes. We won't take what's not ours. We won't desire what other people have. We won't define ourselves by any other thing, and we won't validate ourselves by any other person besides God.

How can we be brought back to life? God gives us the only way that we can respond:

Jeremiah 2:13

> For my people have committed two evils; they have forsaken me the fountain of living waters, and hewed

them out cisterns, broken cisterns, that can hold no water.

Let's just say, generally speaking, if you were successful, if you were accomplished, if you knew your life counted, if you knew you left a legacy, if you knew you were loved, if you knew you left a mark, if you knew your name would live on, would you happy?

What if all these things were true, but no one knew it except you and God? Would you still be happy? Would you be satisfied?

Attempting to find your identity in anything else but God is futile. God is the source of "zoe" life that we desire. Anything else in which we attempt to find life in is not life at all.

We've all tried to dig out our own wells vainly attempting to find life. We're so darkened and our hearts so calloused that we can't even feel that being validated by God is enough.

If we want to be fully alive, then it requires a response. We have forsaken the living waters. We've said that God isn't enough for us. That He's not worth it. That having Him won't satisfy us. We've told Him that we'd rather be validated by other things, other indicators of identity and significance. And we've went out on our own and dug for other sources of life.

Our first response has to be very personally directed to God. Maybe you're honest and you tell God: "I've believed wrongly about You. I just haven't valued You. I haven't believed that You were enough for me. I haven't believed that just having You could possibly satisfy me."

We need to identify the things that have been our false sources of identity and life, and through God's power, we need to fill those wells back up with sand. If you don't know what they are, then ask God to identify them for you. Don't give into fear. Know that He wants to receive you as His child.

Galatians 4:6-7

Because you are sons, God sent the Spirit of His Son into our hearts, the Spirit who calls out, "Abba, Father." So you are no longer a slave, but a son; and since you are a son, God has made you also an heir.

04

all god really wants

UNTIL recently, I'd never come to appreciate the Old Testament. I pretty much assumed that it was just obsolete and there wasn't much to glean from it. I think the majority of Christians feel the same way.

The problem is that the whole of the Old Testament is typically taught as a collection of fabulous stories, a bunch of character studies, an archaic system of practices that Jesus came to take the place of, or a bunch of quips of wisdom that we can readily apply to our life. It is mostly taught in the realm of the concrete, this-is-the-way-it-was or this-is-how-it-happened. The Old Testament is portrayed to be mostly irrelevant for the contemporary Christian.

How does the Old Testament actually read though? It is the story of a starry-eyed Lover who's unwilling to give up on a people He created in His image. Unabashedly and relentlessly, He pursues a people who are at best faithless and unfaithful.

One only has to glance at a single prophecy to find the very words of a God who even in the wake of heartbreak cannot seem to let go, give up, or give in.

Malachi 3:7&17

They will be My people," says the Lord of Heaven's Armies. "On the day when I act in judgment, they will be My own special treasure. I will spare them as a father spares an obedient child.

Ever since the days of your ancestors, you have scorned My decrees and failed to obey them. Now return to Me, and I will return to you"

The entire book is replete with a God who displays a full range of emotions, a God discontent with being distant and unknown.

These bold, raw, in-your-face characteristics stare us in the face and bring us into a deeper knowledge of Him. But, for the most part, we avoid this emotionally charged God. We fear what we cannot understand, but we are more fearful about those things that we can't explain: A jealous God, an angry God, etc. We neuter, dumb-down, oversimplify this wonderful God that desires to be known, and we stick to the safe, common places when we refer to Him.

Listen, He's nuts about you. He's borderline obsessive, and He's not ashamed to tell us that.

The knowledge of God – that tangible knowledge of a Person – is waiting to be pursued. This humble God has shown no restraint in what He would make known about Himself to His people. Most humans are content with only revealing about ourselves what we know won't turn people off. We bring people into a safe proximity where we know we won't be hurt, rejected, and broken. Only those we trust most get into the deepest places.

God chooses to reveal Himself to any who would sincerely seek to know Him. God just seems to me to be this glutton for punishment. Why would God allow flawed, thankless, adulterous people through the ages to repeatedly come close and cause so much personal pain and heartache?

Because He loves us. That's why.

Have you ever thought about the fact that no person has ever experienced unrequited love like God has? He loves in a way that could never possibly be returned. Countless times His creation has walked away from Him. They've been unfaithful. They've chased other things. They've opposed Him. They've cursed Him. They've lived lives independently of Him, pursued things other than Him, blatantly declaring that He is not desirable. These same people don't want their lives infringed upon, but they will quickly shake their fist in His face as soon as things go south in their lives.

And yet, God pursues after us. As a matter of fact, in the moments we were so vehemently opposed to Him, He was constructing a plan. He could see that we could never be faithful. He knew we couldn't possibly fulfill the commitment that was required to be in relationship with Him. So He lowers the bar as much as He possibly could. He makes stepping into a relationship with Him cheap. He makes it free. Of course, it would cost Him everything, but just the chance that He could have us back was worth the risk.

I don't get love like that. God deserves so much better. He has no reason to love us, but He does.

Just a question: what do you think God wants in return? Anytime we get into a relationship with someone there are strings, right? I mean, nothing is really free, is it? Supposedly, God brought us in on a free gift, but the free gift has some kind of requirement doesn't it? Like you'll purchase

10 regularly priced CDs within the next two years or some-thing.

What does God want? Does He want you to serve more?
Give more? Go to church? Manage your sin better? Quit
cheating on your taxes? Make a good boy or girl out of
you? Does He want to impose restrictions on you? Does
He want you feeling guilty now because of everything you've
done wrong in the past? Does He just want you to grovel
because you let Him down?

Ezekiel 11:19

> I will give them one heart, and I will put a new spirit
> within you; and I will take the stony heart out of
> their flesh, and will give them a heart of flesh:

God really only wants one thing. It's all He's ever wanted.
He wants your heart. More simply put, God wants love that
originates there.

Depending on what version of the Bible you use, you can
find anywhere between 750 to 900 instances of the word
"heart."

The Jewish understanding of the heart was that the heart
was the "seat of the emotions." More specifically, in Scripture the heart was seen as the seat of physical life; the seat
of moral nature and spiritual life; the seat of grief and joy;
the desires; the affections; the perceptions; the thoughts
and understanding; the reasoning power; the imagination;
conscience; intentions, purpose and the will; and faith.

Just skimming through Scripture will conjure up vivid ex-
amples of the role of the heart from Pharaoh whose heart
was hardened, to David who was the man "after God's
heart;" even Israel couldn't take their own land that was
promised to them because their hearts were discouraged.

You've probably even heard someone say "I just don't have the heart to do that." Or "My heart won't let me do that." It's true.

The heart is the source of resolve to go on or to quit. It trumps everything.

You can give mental ascent to things. You can know what you're supposed to do. You can believe things with your mind. You can even willpower your way into accomplishing some things or even deny yourself others. But the heart - that passion - it's fuel, unending adrenaline, it's the fight, the bite, the IV drip into the veins of life that thrusts us into doing, being, & walking into who we were made to become.

And when God speaks of the kind of people that He wants and the love that He desires, He always refers to it in no uncertain terms:

> Love Me with your whole heart.
> Their hearts are far from Me.
> Return to the Lord with your whole heart.
> The Lord looks on the heart.
> I will give them one heart.
> You will find Me when you seek Me with your whole heart.

What's so great about love, anyway? What's not great about love?

Love is an incredibly powerful force. Love will send a father into a flaming house to rescue the one he loves. Love will incite a quiet, subdued mother into violence on the behalf of a child who is in danger. Love will cause a man to buy what he cannot afford. Love will make you stay up days at a time, miss meals, endure pain, do illogical things, work 3 jobs, and sacrifice. It has a staying power.

Quite frankly, I Corinthians 13 spells out clearly that any-thing that is not the result of love is nothing. It's empty. It's worthless. God really doesn't want anything that we can "do" for Him. Doing things *for* God or being obedient does not equate love. I can be obedient and follow the rules without ever giving my heart.

Here's the other part of love though: if we truly love God, then out of the overflow of our love comes some really sig-nificant things.

Here's an example:

Let's say I was pulled over by a cop because I wasn't wear-ing my seatbelt. I roll down my window; the cop asks me for my license, registration, and proof of insurance and does the typical battery of questions: Where are you going? Why were you not wearing a seatbelt? Through shiny sun-glasses in a gruff tone he explains the law regarding seatbelts, the penalty of breaking the law, and he gives me "grace" this one time, but warns me not to do it again. Then he wishes me "a nice day" and tells me, "Drive safely."

Even though he let me off the hook, I still believe that he wanted to give me a ticket, because that's what cops do. And I have some friends who are cops, and they really enjoy giving people tickets. They've told me so. The cop wished me a nice day and told me to drive safely. Do I feel warm and fuzzy all over? No, I don't. I still feel under compul-sion. But I pull away having fastened my seatbelt.

What about this scenario? I'm driving down the street with my wife and kids, and I don't have my seatbelt on. My wife asks me, "Why aren't you wearing a seatbelt?" She then goes on to tell me that she's concerned for my well being and that I need to buckle up. You know what I do? I buckle up, not because I know she's right, not because she's trying to run my life, I buckle up because I love my family, and I'd never want to do anything that could risk my future with them.

Both situations seemed to garner the same response didn't they? But I'd have to say that one counted and the other didn't. One was out of legal responsibility; the other was truly out of love. The first will have limitations; it will fail. The second will stand the test of time.

God just wants our love. And if what you do for Him isn't born out of love, then He doesn't want that either.

Do you love God? I mean *really* love Him? I have to confess that I didn't for a really long time. I wanted to go to heaven. I wanted God to do good things for me. I wanted Him to be there when I had a problem or a struggle. I wanted Him to produce, give me answers, bless me, do miraculous stuff and pull me through at the drop of a hat. But I really wasn't interested in having Him.

Besides that, how could you possibly love God? That just seems so out there. He's invisible. He doesn't drink coffee, so that's something that we don't have in common. He's perfect. I'm not.

I think it's difficult to love someone if you don't have a relationship with them. I'd be willing to stick my neck out there and say that if you don't love God, you certainly don't know Him. And God right now is saying to you: "Come and get to know Me."

If you'd dare take the chance, you'll find a God who's gentle and not demanding. He's been so patient up to now; don't you think? He's been so humble and non-threatening. He's never forced Himself. He's never been pushy. He's never put you on a guilt trip.

You know this is all true. Maybe you think that you can't love God. Maybe you know how limited and failing your love is. Scripture has a beautiful story of this very exchange between God and man.

John 21:15 – 17

> So when they had eaten breakfast, Jesus said to
> Simon Peter, "Simon, son of Jonah, do you love Me
> more than these?"
> He said to Him, "Yes, Lord; You know that I love
> You."
> He said to him, "Feed my lambs."
> He said to him again a second time, "Simon, son of
> Jonah, do you love Me?"
> He said to Him, "Yes, Lord; you know that I love
> You."
> He said to him, "Tend my sheep."
> He said to him the third time, "Simon, son of Jonah,
> do you love Me?" Peter was grieved because He said
> to him the third time, "Do you love Me?"
> And he said to Him, "Lord, You know all things; You
> know that I love You."

Peter was a disciple. This whole conversation is taking
place within 40 days of Peter's meltdown. Do you remember that? Jesus is in the Garden of Gethsemane. Judas is
on his way with the Roman soldiers and when all those
guys show up Jesus is pretty much abandoned by everybody. Peter had already told Jesus: "Jesus, I will die for
you." But like Jesus predicted, he denied his connection
with Jesus 3 times. Verse 62 of Luke tells of how Peter
went off and boo-hooed like never before.

I can imagine Peter was like: "I was supposed to be different. I'm a failure! He told me I was going to deny Him, and
I told Him convincingly that I would be there for Him and I
failed. I let Him down. I can't do this life!"

And so Jesus catches up with Peter and this extraordinary
exchange happens between Peter and Jesus that focuses on
Peter's love for Him. So many times when I read this I
thought: "Wow, that must have been difficult. It was a personal confrontation. And Jesus seems to be upping the
ante on what He requires of His followers. He's asking Pe-

ter if he loves Him." Honestly, I was uncomfortable with the passage because I knew if Jesus asked me I couldn't have responded, "Yes, I love you."

I misunderstood thinking Jesus kept asking Peter the same question because Peter didn't really love Him. But what I learned on closer study was the inadequacy of the English language to convey this conversation.

When Jesus first asks Peter, "Do you love me?" The word that for love that he used was the word: "Agapao." Agapao speaks of a love which is awakened by a sense of value in the object loved. It's a selfless, sacrificial love of choice. It's not a love based on what one can get out of it. It is the love of perfection – literally the kind of love God had for His Son and for His creation.

So Jesus asks Peter, "Do you *Agapo* me?"

And Peter responds: "Yes, Lord; you know that I love you." Of course, the word that Peter used for love was not "Agapo." He responded with a different kind of love. The word Peter used was the word "Phileo." Phileo was a love of friendly affection. It is a love called out of one in response to a feeling of pleasure or delight. It is love, but not perfect love.

A second time, Jesus asks: "Peter, Do you Agapo me?" Peter responds again, "Yes, Lord; you know that I *Phileo* you."

If I'm Peter, I'm kinda sweating this right now.

And now comes the the third line of questioning, but in this question, Jesus does a little switch.

Jesus asks: "Peter, do you *Phileo* Me."

Peter is broken and he replied, "You know me. You know the depth of my heart. You know I *Phileo* you."

39

Why the switch? I think what we're seeing is the gentleness of God made evident by Jesus here. Jesus was making it abundantly clear that He loved Peter, selflessly, relentlessly, sacrificially, as though Peter was a precious treasure. Peter honestly couldn't have loved Jesus that way. He knew that was the love of perfection, so he responded as honestly as he could: "Jesus, I don't love You like *that*, but I love you *this* much."

And Jesus' asking the question again seemed to restate His love for Peter despite Peter's weakness to love Him back, while stressing the fact that God truly desires to be deeply loved.

But the third time, Jesus changes the question. He asks the question in such a way that Peter becomes unhinged. I don't think Peter was grieved because he thought that Jesus didn't believe him, I think he realized the kind of love he was receiving and that he just couldn't meet it with an adequate kind of love.

And you know what Jesus was saying? He was saying to Peter, "That's enough for Me right now. Your love isn't perfect, but it'll do. I'll receive your love."

I think that's what God desires to say to you right now. When you say: "God, I can't love you because I don't know You yet." Or "God I like you as a friend." Or "God, I love You, but I know I don't love You enough." God responds with an "I'll receive your love. Whatever expression it is right now, as incomplete and weak as you think it is, I want it."

When I think of God responding like that, it causes me to become undone. It makes me love Him. It compels me to want to know Him more. It makes me wonder what He could possibly see in me; why my love could matter so much to Him; how a huge God like He is could be moved and thrilled by what little I give Him in return.

Do you think maybe you could respond to God right now?

If God told you, "I love you fully, completely, unconditionally, and sacrificially. Do you love Me?"

How do you respond to that? Respond to Him right now the best you know how.

And God says, "I *still* love you fully, completely, unconditionally, and sacrificially. I'm ecstatic and thrilled to receive your love for Me. Whatever you've got, I'll take it!"

05

knowing god

My friend Bobby and I were talking one day, and he told me how it is amazing the amount of money, time, and preparation that's expended to put together a wedding – a single day, a single event that no one usually remembers and that may last a sum total of 6 hours including the reception (those are the really good Catholic ones of course!). He went on to say that in comparison for the preparation for the actual marriage – the lifelong commitment – there is hardly any thought or discussion.

And he's right. People just assume that with their 1 mandatory visit with the pastor or priest that somehow everything's just going to fall in place. They'll figure it out. Marriage isn't rocket science, right?

I think we all know what the marriage statistic is in the U.S. Young couples should know: love is difficult, commitment is hard. It hurts to prefer another person above yourself. Some days you won't like your spouse, and you still have to sacrifice for them.

I find it fascinating that in the Bible there is so much of a focus on the heart with a strong allusion to marriage that just keeps coming up all throughout the Book.

Idolatry was equated with adultery, and even we, as Christians, are known as the "bride of Christ."

No one ever prepared us to be in this kind of a relationship with God. Some people tried to tell us how to go about it, which typically looked like someone throwing a Bible at us, telling us to go to church often, or to take part in a small group. Again, it was a lot of activity, but it didn't equate with growing in a deeper personal knowledge of God.

WE KNOW A LOT...

Our favorite pastime as human beings is talking about people. We're fascinated by people.

I crack up when I catch my wife watching TMZ, Talk Soup, and some of these other celeb shows. If you watch those things enough, you can convince yourself that you know these people. You can know who's fighting with who, where they bought their dress, what their driving record is – there is a lot of information out there that makes us smart fans. We can fool others and even convince ourselves about how much we know, but that's a far cry from actually knowing someone.

A lot of our knowledge of people in our social circles is second hand at best. It's not even our experience. When we have a fun experience with people, we tell everyone.

When we have conflict with people, we go to close friends, family, or spouses to help process what happened. Who are these people? Are they just jerks? Or am I the jerk?

Sometimes we have bad first impressions of people that always linger as an underlying belief about them. Sometimes people tell us their impression of someone and we belief falsely about them. It will even lead us to avoidance. Sometimes we're even surprised to find that our first impressions are wrong. The individual turns out to be someone completely different. "Hey, she's not an airhead." or "This whole time I thought he didn't like me."

No matter what people say, no matter what our first impressions are, no matter what the rumor mill is, no matter what the tabloid headlines read, everything that there is to know about a person – the information – is forced to submit to our personal experiences of them. That is what is real for us.

The people you know best in life are the people that you have chosen to love. Maybe it's your mom, or your dad, or your child. Can you take 3 solid minutes to describe the person you love the most in the world?

Try it.

And where did all that knowledge come from? It came from experience. We have seen, felt, shared, conversed, walked, talked, laughed, cried, celebrated, endured, suffered, and it's led to an intimate knowledge of them.

Let me stop right here and ask you another question. Who is God? Can you take a solid 3 minutes and describe Him to me?

Just try it.

Is it different from the way you described the person you described a few moments ago? It usually is. Why? Because we haven't seen, felt, shared, conversed, walked, talked, laughed, cried, celebrated, endured, or suffered with God. If we describe God with grandiose terms, and we haven't truly experienced Him that way, then it's not real knowledge. If we know God as harsh, oppressive, or displeased with us, then we have to ask ourselves: "Where did I pick

44

up this knowledge of God? Did I legitimately experience this for myself?"

The source of our knowledge is the biggest problem. It's second or third hand at best. We live vicariously through other people's experiences, their thoughts, their impressions. We know a lot about God, but that doesn't translate to truly *knowing* Him. Sometimes it even damages us. It may even cause us to avoid Him. We read stuff. We hear stuff, but we don't typically come close.

Why are we okay with second hand knowledge of God when He desires for us to come close? Part of it may very well be that we just don't see the worth in Him. We make time, we pursue things that matter most to us. When Paul spoke of knowing God, he discovered the value of that knowledge to be priceless.

Philippians 3:8-9

> Yes, furthermore, I count everything as loss compared to the possession of the priceless privilege (the overwhelming preciousness, the surpassing worth, and supreme advantage) of knowing Christ Jesus my Lord and of progressively becoming more deeply and intimately acquainted with Him [of perceiving and recognizing and understanding Him more fully and clearly]. For His sake I have lost everything and consider it all to be mere rubbish (refuse, dregs), in order that I may win (gain) Christ (the Anointed One), And that I may [actually] be found and known as in Him...

I started traveling from time to time shortly after our second child was born. It was really difficult being out of town during Jadyn's formative developmental years. I loved calling home and asking how the baby was doing, but I hated it at the same time. It seemed that in every conversation, Jessica would tell me something new that Jadyn was doing. I was excited for Jadyn, but I honestly was disappointed that I'd missed it. I have to admit that I was jealous of Jessica for being there to experience it. Sure, I could come home and see her doing it again, but I'd missed the moment.

Sometimes people will babysit our kids and tell us what we're missing when we call home. I'm glad they're enjoying my kids, but I'm so dissatisfied with hearing about it. *I* want to have that experience.

I think it's time for us to be dissatisfied. God desires to be known. He *is* great. He *is* mighty, powerful, patient, merciful, loving, satisfying, and all of those things we've heard, but we'll never know until we experience Him for ourselves.

HOW DO WE PURSUE KNOWLEDGE ?

I find it ironic that this process of getting to know God is often in the context of something many Christians in America commonly know as "Sunday School."

If I think of it in modernistic terms, it's academic, schoolbook knowledge. If I tell someone to gain knowledge about something, they usually will ask someone who is an expert, go to the library, read a book, or surf the web and grab it. Wikipedia, podcasts, Youtube and many sources abound. Bam! It's done.

This is the way we we're usually taught in church, and there's a huge problem with that.

Take a look at Paul's prayer in Ephesians again:

Ephesians 3:17-19

I pray that out of His glorious riches He may strengthen you with power through His Spirit in your inner being, so that Christ may dwell in your hearts through faith. And I pray that you, being rooted and established in love, may have power, together with

46

all the saints, to grasp how wide and long and high and deep is the love of Christ, and to know this love that surpasses knowledge—that you may be filled to the measure of all the fullness of God.

This word know again in this passage is the Greek word "ginosko." Here's the unpacking of that term:

- to learn to know, come to know, get a knowledge of perceive, feel
- to become known
- to know, understand, perceive, have knowledge of
- to understand
- to become fully acquainted with, to know
- to acknowledge
- Jewish idiom for sexual intercourse between a man and a woman

The deeper we get into this word, we come to the reality that spiritual transformation is incomplete until we come to an intimate knowing of God comparable to a husband knowing his wife.

The knowledge that Adam and Eve lost at the fall was not academic. It was relational. Relationship was intrinsic to knowledge. And you know what? Relationship is still instrinsic to knowledge. Nothing has changed.

Well, actually something has changed – namely, us! We've been changed by God. When we began a relationship with Jesus, a work took place in our hearts. Where we once separated from God, we now find Jesus inviting us to "come learn of Him." Where our hearts were once darkened to the knowledge of God, the veil that once covered our hearts has been removed. We've now been given the "mind of Christ," and we have His Spirit – the essence of Jesus Himself – to speak, to make Him known, and affirm in hearts who He is and who we are. We possess everything there is to truly know Him.

What does that look like in practice though?

I'm extremely careful with this question because it can so quickly lead to formulas and insincerity. There are steps to everything these days. Steps to prayer, steps to a better you, steps to getting what you want from God. It's selfish and dishonest. How insincere would it come off if on the next date you're on, you ran that person through a formulated process in order to "get to know them?" You think they'd hate that? You think anyone would want that? Of course not. It's at best contrived and unnatural.

How does getting to know a person happen in any relationship? Since we're talking about a relationship that is comparable to marriage, maybe there are some cues that can help us:

Ask the basic questions. Ask the really tough questions. Ask anything you want. This isn't a theology lesson, mind you, it's getting to know a Person. What's it going to take to make this relationship survive? How do you really know God loves you? Do you love Him? If God loves you, what does that mean for the choices in your life? What are your pet peeves? What are God's pet peeves?

Share your struggles. Share your first impressions. Tell Him why you're angry with Him. Tell Him the picture that you have of Him and ask Him to reveal Himself if there's anything inaccurate about it. Share what the tabloids say about Him. Talk to God about the conflict someone else has with Him.

Invite Him along the ride for each and every moment of your life. Talk to Him about the things you've been avoiding. Tell God a joke. Share the beauty of nature with Him beside you. Have regular alone moments. Go out on dates. Never break from conversation.

Now, go back to the things that you used to do with this different heart. Read the Bible to know Him. Consider those words to be living and breathing spoken by the Author who's living inside you. Don't get in marathon reading contests. Stop as He speaks. Interact with Him.

Pray. But don't let it be one-sided. Let God respond. Don't even consider the notion that God might not respond. God didn't begin this relationship with you to generally guide you, to tease you by leaving some of His encrypted writings that would leave you dumbfounded as to their meaning, or to watch from a distance as you performed various acts in an attempt to appease Him. He speaks. He wants you to know His voice.

Ask God to help you know the height, depth, width, and length of His love. Go back to church to experience His presence with other followers. Attend that small group and share your first-hand experiences of God. Challenge what you don't know to be true in your heart.

What happens when God is truly known? What happens when God's love is an experience rather than a cliché? What happens when God shows up in the picture moment by moment? What happens when your relationship becomes more than just a Person in your life, but He becomes part of your identity? What happens when this Person is so tightly wrapped up in your being?

My opinion? I think you become ONE. I think what the other Person thinks matters. I think the other Person comes up a lot – in every decision. I think you feel as ONE. You come to share the same thoughts as that Person. You finish His sentences.

And after you come to know Him, commit to never figuring Him out again.

I know that if I ever figure my wife out, if I ever stop discovering and re-discovering her, then our relationship is as good as dead.

Paul calls God "unsearchable". It doesn't mean that we can't know Him; it's that there is so much to Him that our finite minds could never know everything. Just when you think that you've figured Him out, you find another door that opens you to another dimension. Complexity isn't frustrating. It's beautiful. It keeps us curious and our passion stirred.

Are you curious now? Is your passion stirred? Then go: Find Him. Know Him. Experience Him.

06

mirrors

WHAT A MIRROR CAN TELL YOU...

As a favor to people, I always discreetly tell them if they have some obstruction like sleep in their eye, lipstick on their teeth, food in their beard, etc. In my opinion, it should be a common courtesy.

Several years back, it was my friend Nick's wedding day. I was best man, so that gives you a lot of privileges like backstage access to the food at the reception even hours before the food can legally be consumed. It also puts you in charge of the groom like, being a gopher, dealing with last minute details so that he doesn't have to stress, and, of course, making sure he shows up.

The day of the wedding was going very smoothly. I was giving him a ride to the wedding and making small talk so that he remained at ease. As we were talking, I was noticing something in the corner of my eye. It was enough to gain my attention that I kept looking at him as I was driving.

Suddenly I shrieked, "Holy cow, Nick! You've got nose hairs sticking out of your left nostril!"

"What?" Nick responded with a confused look on his face and grabbed the rearview mirror turning it his direction so that he could make a keen observation. "Oh, it's not that bad."

"What do you mean 'it's not that bad?' It looks like you've got a Granddaddy Longlegs stuck up your nose. You gotta do something about that thing!"

Nick didn't have any tweezers on him. What man does? So he's pushing up the left side of his nose to expose the middle shaft of the nosehair while creating a larger space for his thumb and index finger.

I did what I could to help and lend moral support. I even pulled out my Panasonic Camcorder – not the small kind either – to document the event. All the while, I'm trying to drive down I-10 in New Orleans.

After numerous unsuccessful attempts at pluckage, we finally made it to the hall, and the best man was forced to lead a covert operation of looking for tweezers for the groom. I'm happy to say that I successfully tracked down a pair; the follicles were removed; the wedding went on as planned, and they lived happily ever after.

Mirrors are great aren't they? Most bathrooms have them, because those periodic moments in the day are great, convenient times to take a closer look and see what the rest of the world is seeing when you're not looking. They can show you flaws that sometimes you're not even aware of.

But do you know what mirrors are really bad at doing? In Nick's case, it could show him the nosehair protruding out of his nostril; it could help him locate it, but it was terrible at helping him remove it. That's not really surprising is it? I mean, we all know what the function of a mirror is.

I love the fact that in James 1:23, the writer uses this powerful imagery of a mirror.

> Anyone who listens to the word [or in this Scriptural context, you could use the words "law," "rules," "Christian morals," or "principles"] and does not do what is says is like a man who looks at his face in a mirror, and after looking at himself, goes away and forgets what he looks like.

Here's the way that I understand this: Rules or Christian values act like a mirror. They can show you something in your life that needs to be changed, but they can't clean you up. It doesn't matter how well you follow the rules, they can never change who you are inside.

Of course, if you've been in church for any length of time, we sure do talk about those things like they are the priority. Like they still really mean something. And as much as they've been talked about, shoved in our face and down our throats, the lives of Christians are still going down the toilet.

A lot of Christians on the whole don't feel a whole lot different than they did in their pre-Christian days. They struggle with the same things that used to beat them over the head in the old days. Morally, they're pretty much the same as well. I was up close and personal with this reality for most of my days working in youth ministry. Some 80% of teenagers walk away from church by the time they graduate from high school. It's been the dirty little secret of youth ministry for years. Christian teenagers lie as much, drink as much, and have sex as much as non-Christians. There's almost no moral difference.

Honestly though, I don't think their parents are any better. There is just as much porn addiction, infidelity, and an even higher divorce rate among Christian adults as non-Christians.

The answer that the Church has had is blaming immoral culture. Let's blast the culture because of all its evil influences. Let's vote on resolutions to ban same-sex marriages; let's protest the removal of the 10 Commandments in Alabama. We're losing America because we've lost our morals. Let's teach kids to defend their faith. Let's send them off on mission trips; get them *doing* more things.

It's not working, is it? And that's because the basic design of the law was never meant to change anyone, nor was it to make more committed followers of Christ.

Long before we knew Jesus and the Holy Spirit, God instituted something that we've come to know as the law. The law – this standard for being righteous (or "right") in God's eyes wasn't a bad thing. But its purpose was never really to make people in right standing with God. Instead, it was supposed to show us our dire need *for* God. As Paul put it, the law "was our schoolmaster to bring us unto Christ."

Stepping into a relationship with Jesus was supposed to be the beginning of experiencing freedom. It was never meant to re-introduce nor re-impose the law on us. America will not be saved by Christian values. The law doesn't save people. Jesus does. Rules will not create more committed followers of Christ because it is powerless to change people. Only Jesus can change people.

What we are talking about here really is a basic heart issue isn't it? And that change can only occur through a relationship with Jesus. The problem is that the primary relationship that that we as Christians have is with a set of morals, values, disciplines, a system of interpretive rules and traditions, and even with a Book rather than with a Person.

Law is weak and unfulfilling. One might wonder why we would pursue it rather than running after God. I think it's because it's a lot easier to conform and adapt to a list of rules than it is to commit to a relationship with a person.

THE KITCHEN CABINETS OF LIFE

I honestly believe that the change that God chose to bring in our lives as Christians was not so that we would have longer lists and thicker, darker, Marks-a-lot boundaries in our lives. In fact, as I walk this thing out, I see Jesus taking an eraser to the boundaries in my life and eliminating the lines that were once drawn either by religious law or the compulsion of other people.

When I say stuff like God taking away boundaries, it always makes people nervous. Some people get defensive and angry. To some, it's borderline heresy. "God's not going to take the boundaries off our lives. The rules are good. We're just bad."

Let me clarify this: I'm not saying that there is no black and white when it comes to moral behavior. I'm also not saying that we can just go out and live how we please.

We're so uncomfortable with all the gray areas in the Bible that we often feel it necessary to draw these bold, dark lines around things, so we don't screw up.

Much more than right and wrong, we're even more uncomfortable with our responsibility to choose. Let's face it: most of life is gray, so God really left a lot of empty blanks when it came to living it.

I think about our kids when they were little and in the "gettin' into everything" stage. If you're not a parent yet, it's the stage when a child first gets mobile and you line everything with a 3-inch thick strip of grey foam, put breakables at least 4 feet high, and you use these inconvenient little clips on your kitchen cabinets that cause adults more personal

injury mashing fingers than they probably have ever pre-
vented.

Child-proofing a house is no way to live. It's a stressful,
deliberate action. As a parent, you long for the day when
your child no longer desires to open a cabinet and drink
toxic chemicals.

I think that's a perfect picture of where God chooses to
bring us. Rather than running prevention programs and
legislating morality, God knew the only way to truly change
what we were doing was to change our hearts. If our hearts
were changed, then our desires would be changed.

How would God do this? Well, not to be terribly repetitive,
He began this work with love. In Romans 2:4, it says that it
is God's loving kindness that leads to repentance. We
change our minds and do what's right because we are
loved.

God believed that if He could infiltrate people's hearts, if
people really knew how He felt about them, if they experienced His love, they would change.

But God didn't stop there; He wasn't done working inside
the heart.

Jeremiah 31:33

> But this shall be the covenant that I will make with
> the house of Israel; I will put My law in their inward
> parts, and write it in their hearts; and I will be their
> God, and they shall be My people.

It's better than law that goes out of style or seemingly needs
amendments and updates, God chose to literally write His
law into the very hearts of His people. He no longer needed
to lock things down to keep us out of trouble. He would
remind us in our very being.

Jessica and I have this deal as husband and wife that if I ever say or do anything stupid in public that she'll let me know in a very subtle, gentle way. This was my wife's suggestion, because she always wanted to be respectful even when I make a mistake in the presence of other people. We've grown to know each other so well over the years that I can tell by a certain look on her face that's undetectable by the common person. Sometimes I'm not that aware, and Jessica will gently lay her hand on my leg or grab my hand.

I've noticed that God works in very much the same way with me. Rather than beating me over the head or berating me, there is a gentle impression on my heart of not just wrong but what is the right thing to do.

But God doesn't stop there, because what is the law except for a mirror? It examines us, but it is powerless to change us. Here's how God works that out in us:

Ezekiel 11:19

And I will give them one heart, and I will put a new spirit within you; and I will take the stony heart out of their flesh, and will give them a heart of flesh...

God gives us a new heart with His law – the ability to see and know right and wrong – and He places within our hearts His Spirit.

John 6:63

It is the Spirit who gives life...

We are unable to change ourselves. Sometimes God shows us the things that we are supposed to do and even avoid and honestly, we are powerless on our own to do the right thing. He doesn't leave us alone. He doesn't call us to be a different kind of people and leave us powerless to act on it. Instead He infuses us with His power – the same power that enabled Christ to live through temptation, heal people, defeat Satan, and overcome even death – God's Spirit is power. It is access for us to become people that we never could have become on our own.

07

grace

BREAKING FREE

SEVERAL years ago, I was coerced into going with a group of guys to a men's retreat in Hot Springs, Arkansas. My friend Steve had instituted this sort of Mecca for a number of guys around our church. I talked to a few of the guys who'd been going for years about what it was like, and they all gave me raving reviews about the experience. I have to admit they were pretty convincing, and the brochure was a fairly slick marketing piece that had a man's hands breaking free of chains. I knew there were a few things I needed help dealing with, so maybe this would be worth it.

The first night of the event, the retreat leader Tim dove right in. He was brash, honest, to the point, and blunt to say the least. He told us that we men had a lot of issues that we needed to identify in our lives like: lust, pornography, drinking beer, and playing fantasy football. It was time to examine ourselves and deal with these issues "once and for all." We were going to walk out of that retreat set free.

I like most of the men there were like, "Sign me up." To start this process, Tim handed out blank hospital bracelets and Sharpies to the group of 200 or so men. He told us to write our struggles on the bracelets, then flip the writing face side down and snap it onto our wrists. He said we needed to be constantly reminded of our issue.

Shortly after that first session was over, our group of guys reconvened. Danny, a heavyset, George Costanza look-a-like walked up to me with elation on his face and said, "I'm going to get set free from everything this weekend." He held up his arms; both of his chubby wrists were bearing at least 13 of those hospital bracelets, and his hands were already turning purple.

Session after session passed. In each one, Tim drove home the point that our sins were serious issues that needed to be resolved. We needed to admit and confront them.

Following session 72 on this 3 day retreat, I was too exhausted to leave my plastic lawnchair for the 15 minute break in between floggings. My friend Brian was sitting next to me looking just as exhausted. He looked around nervously as though there might be a rat who would turn him in, and when the coast was clear, he leaned over and said: "Well, Paul, what do you think?"

I said, "I feel like I've had the hell beat out of me, but I'm afraid I'm no different than when I walked in here. I know what my issues are. I know they're bad. I don't want them. But there's no application here except that *I* need to *do* something about it."

The final evening of the retreat finally rolled around. The finality of all the brow-beating was that it was decision-making time. Did we want to continue struggling and living in sin or did we want to break free? The moment of truth is now. At the conclusion of the session, Tim directed us to a bonfire down the hill. Jesus would be waiting for us there -

next to the cross. If we were ready to give up our struggle (that we apparently still liked), then we could walk down the hill to Jesus and leave our bracelet with Him.

I got up and walked to the congested exit and joined the other cattle who were being herded towards the cross. I walked up to Jesus who was standing a few feet away from a 10 foot tall cross. Jesus slipped a pair of scissors out of the sleeve of His robe, snipped my bracelet, and I tossed it into the fire.

I walked up the hill and sat on bench with profound sadness as I watched man after man walk up to Jesus to have their struggle removed. I thought about my George Constanza friend and wondered if he would really be able to kick his smoking habit when he got home. The burden had been placed on these whipped, broken men to change.

The entire scene was summed up by the conversation of two guys who walked past me in the shadows.

First guy: "Are you free now?"
Second guy: "I guess so. Jesus did His part; now I've got to do mine."

That conversation just cut me. It hurt me as deeply then as it does now just recalling it. It was the conversation of this man's heart, and it's a reflection of the heart of most Christians who still live in their struggles.

Jesus did *His* part; now we have to do *ours*.

I believed that for a really long time. I quit trying to follow Jesus for years, effectively walking away, not because I didn't believe in Him, but because I was tired of failing. I knew He'd done His part in bringing me into a relationship with God, but I couldn't manage to keep my end of the deal. I just couldn't change.

Is that the deal God made with us though? He gives you grace to enable you to step into a relationship with Him. That's *His* end? Go out and do right. Live above sin and do great works for Him. Is that how you understand *your* end?

I'm not sure where we came up with that, because Scripture doesn't reflect this kind of arrangement at all.

Ezekiel 11:19

And I will give them one heart, and I will put a new spirit within you; and I will take the stony heart out of their flesh, and will give them a heart of flesh...

God said that he was going to give us new hearts. Our new hearts would be alive to God. We would experience His love, be changed, and realize our identity. His law would be etched into our hearts. We would despise wrong and desire right. And God completes His work in us by grace – unending favor – by the power of His Spirit.

When we were dead to God and unable to save ourselves, Jesus stepped in to do what we could not on our own. But what God began in bringing us into relationship with Him, He has to finish. Absent from the power of Christ in us, we are still weak.

What Jesus began, only *He* can finish.

RELATIONAL CHANGE

Jesus explained this relational dynamic between Himself and us through a vine and branches metaphor.

John 15:4

Abide in Me, and I in you. As the branch cannot bear fruit of itself, unless it abides in the Vine, neither can you unless you abide in Me. I am the Vine, you are the branches. He who abides in Me, and I in

him, bears much fruit; for without Me, you can do
nothing.

Jesus tells us to remain in Him because He is the Vine.
And there's a really good reason for that – we cannot produce on our own. Jesus even restates it: "You guys are just
branches. Branches don't produce on their own!"

Imagine how stupid a person would be if they wanted to
produce grapes, and they walked into the field of a winery,
pulled out a machete and hacked off a branch thinking
they could bring it home and produce their own grapes.
Should they be surprised a week later to find the branch
dried up, withered, and producing nothing?

I don't think that we fully grasp our relationship with Jesus. The beginning of our relationship with Him began
with our dependence on Him to do what we couldn't do
ourselves. Trying to live above sin, "breaking free," living
victoriously, thriving, changing, transforming, is only possible through this vital connection. We are dependent on
Jesus to enable these things to happen. We don't walk up
to Jesus and thank Him for what He *did*, and say "now *I'm*
going to change." In that very moment, we disconnect ourselves from the life-giving Power that enables change to
take place.

I believe that we need to break free. We need to be deliv-
ered. I think we have a number of our own vices that are
holding us down. I also think that a lot of issues of sin are
not just our own. There is sin that was committed against
us. People who struggle with doubt, frustration, anxiety,
anger, depression – these are real struggles that we have to
be set free from. We can't just suck it up and go on with
our lives. Willpower, self-denial, positive thinking, "pull
ourselves up by our bootstraps" – all of these things are
what they Bible calls "works of the flesh." It denies grace.
It invalidates and makes a mockery out of what Jesus did
at the cross. It denies our need for God. It cuts us off and
separates us from His power.

RELATIONAL WORKS

I often ask people, "How are things going in your relationship with God?" I tell them to give me a rating on a scale of 1 to 10, 10 being the highest. Most of the responses are varied. The answers are always based on what they are doing. For instance, some person might say, "I'd give myself a 4 because I haven't read my Bible much lately." Another person might say, "I'd give myself a 6 because I've been going to church every week, but I haven't been praying enough.

In Galatians 5:22, Paul provides us a much better indicator of how that relationship is going:

> ...the fruit of the Spirit is love, joy, peace, longsuffering, kindness, goodness, faithfulness, gentleness, self-control.

Works aren't indicators of life. That's an old system that denies grace.

If our relationship with God is going well, then we should see something. We should see fruit. You know what fruit is an indicator of? It's an indicator of life. Only things that are alive can produce fruit, right? But what produces fruit? Do we produce fruit? No, we don't. Fruit is produced by the Spirit.

So follow this with me: if we are vitally connected to God in relationship, fruit will be produced. If we're not, then nothing will be produced. But even what is produced is not because we worked it up and made it happen. Remember what Jesus said: without *Me* you can do *nothing*.

WHAT ABOUT FAITH?

I find it interesting that we call Christians believers and we call non-Christians nonbelievers. Often we're one in the same though.

Have you ever noticed how difficult it is to "just believe" or to "just have faith?" It's tough. We beat our brains out trying to convince ourselves or other people for that matter to trust or believe in God.

I don't advocate checking out your brain to believe in Jesus, but here's the problem with faith – it always falls a little short when it comes to explaining things. There is going to be a place where our knowledge is incomplete. We have a deep sense that something is true, but we don't have tangible evidence. That's faith. It's the felt experience of the reality of something without being able to see it.

I appreciate people who are highly analytical and brainy. For them we have a whole system of apologetics – meant to give more scientific answers as to why we believe what we believe. But there's a fundamental problem with all this convincing and proving. It's that belief in Jesus – faith – doesn't happen in your mind, it happens in your heart.

When it comes to faith in Jesus, our hearts know something that our mind does not. The mind can be changed; we can be convinced of things, but only after the heart has been changed first.

A great example of this is in Mark 9, when a man with a demonized son brings him to Jesus for deliverance. Jesus responds to him by saying, "all things are possible to him who believes." And the man responds with a paradox: "I believe; help my unbelief!"

Doesn't that sound just like us? We believe, but we need help with our unbelief.

65

In Romans 1, Paul described thinking as futile. There is all this living proof of God, but until the heart is brought back to life and illuminated by God, it's impossible to believe.

It's difficult to admit unbelief isn't it? Especially when you're supposed to *be* a believer.

HOW DO YOU BECOME A BELIEVER?

Long before he became world famous on the internet as "The Fart Preacher," Robert Tilton had a highly profitable daily broadcast called "Success N' Life." On this show the 800 number would be permanently affixed across the bottom of the TV screen while Tilton encouraged people to make a "vow of faith" – make a promise to God with the exercise of it being your financial gift to the ministry.

As this story has been highly documented by the press as criminal usury, it still underscores a common belief among Christians – that faith is an effort on our part to move God into action on our behalf.

If you *do* this.
If you *claim* it.
If you *speak* it.
If you *give* money.
If *you...*

We've applied this action to everything from healing to finances. But what is faith? Is it just an action?

Growing up in church, they used to do this two-person faith illustration. One person would stand in front of another. The first person would be told to just fall backwards without trying to catch himself in total reliance on the other to catch him.

Most people would try to catch themselves - at least a little bit. Our teacher would always point out that they tried to catch themselves because they didn't have any faith, which was somewhat inaccurate. What was faith based on? Is it based on something you could work up or something you could sike yourself up into believing? No, faith is based on *relationship*.

Little people who would just fall backwards would always get praised as people with a lot of faith, while the biggest person in the room would be chided as being weak because they'd always chicken out and catch themselves. It made sense to our feeble minds then, but we today cannot keep going on like the little person produced some kind of superhuman faith.

The illustration was relational. The first part of relationship is whether or not this guy actually *wants* to catch me. Is he a good guy? Would he let me fall just to get a laugh at me? If I can't trust him, at some point I'm going to try to catch myself.

But let's say you don't know the guy that well. You look him over, and the only thing you know to do is make a comparison. If I'm bigger than him, it doesn't matter how nice of a guy he is, I'm hitting the ground. If we're the same size, I'm still not that confident. But if I'm little, and he's big, then maybe I can just fall and be caught.

When the little guy in class dropped without thinking twice about it, we really shouldn't have been so blown away. He understood the relationship between himself and the catcher. It was an accurate response to relationship, not some great human feat.

In the New Testament, the Greek word for faith that we often see used is the word "Pistis."

The word stresses relationship of knowing the character of God. Because I know the character of God, I know that I can trust Him. If I don't know God, then I can't trust Him. If I'm not convinced that God loves me despite my own flaws, then there's a chance He won't catch me. If I don't think God is good, then maybe God will let me drop just to have the enjoyment of seeing me fall.

All of this is born out of knowledge. Where knowledge of God is incomplete, we're going to be short on faith. It makes sense that we try to catch ourselves, because we don't know God well enough to just drop.

There are some people we know who just fall on a whim for God. We struggle with that in ourselves because we know we've never been able to do that. We regard those people as "people with faith" while we apparently have none.

I know a guy named Bob Obert, and everywhere that Bob goes he prays for someone to be healed. And you know what happens? A lot of people are healed. Bob has outrageous even impossible stories about God.

Me? I have a few. I believe God heals, and I pray for people. I've been a part of some cool stories, but I'd say overall it's been a lot more miss than hit. What's the difference between Bob and I?

I don't think Bob is a faith healer. I don't believe Bob heals people. And Bob doesn't think that either. Why does it happen so much around Bob? It's because Bob prays for everybody. He prays for people to be healed probably a hundred times more than I do. He does it because he has this knowledge of a loving God who desires to heal people. He was healed of a drug addiction cold turkey some 25 years ago. This is an intimate, very personal understanding of God, and it thrusts him to act on what he knows. For him, it's not some giant faith feat on his part. He's responding to God in the way that he knows Him.

Me? I want to know God like that. I'd have to admit that I've prayed very half-heartedly for people most of my life, because I really wasn't convinced that God wanted to heal people. Besides that, I thought it had something to do with me and my faith. My efforts always fell short, so I knew my faith would.

Faith is relational. We respond in trust with God according to how we know God.

But there's another way we respond. When we stepped into this relationship with Jesus, we had no knowledge of Him at all. We couldn't have been more darkened in our knowledge of God. But something happened. What was it?

We recognized God as God and ourselves as frail human beings. It wasn't some great feat of faith to begin a relationship with God, it was admitting our weakness, our smallness compared to God. As long as God is bigger than us, we can fall and know we're going to be caught. That's how relationship with God always begins.

How does our faith increase? It increases as our knowledge of God increases. Our knowledge of God is still dark in a lot of places. We've not seen God's character tested in places we've never been with Him before.

FEAR

I have a friend of mine that told me that fear is going to be ever-present and we have to have courage to move in spite of it.

I sort of agreed.

Is fear going to be ever-present? I think it is, but it was never God's intention.

Going back to the Adam and Eve story, fear was the first emotion experienced after the heart of God and the heart of man and woman was broken. When this brokenness happened, knowledge of God was lost. They feared loneliness and judgment. We still fear loneliness, judgment, and even rejection to this day.

God never wanted that.

I John 4:18

There is no fear in love. But perfect love drives out fear, because fear has to do with punishment. The one who fears is not made perfect in love.

Where there is still fear in us, it is where we our hearts have not been illuminated by God's love. Where there is love, there is no fear. They can't co-exist.

If we still fear, then we still don't fully know God's love. God isn't okay with our not knowing His love. He will always bring us to places where our knowledge of His love is incomplete, where we have to fall, be caught, and be embraced by His love. That's the work that faith really does. We know God more fully, and He's able to embrace us. We know a freedom that we've never known.

FAITH IS A GIFT

Hebrews 11:6

And without faith it is impossible to please God, because anyone who comes to Him must believe that He exists and that He rewards those who earnestly seek Him.

I used to really struggle with this Scripture. My best guess was that God simply wasn't pleased with me because I didn't have any faith. I still doubted. I'd never *proven* my faith. I couldn't even bring myself to send $25 to Robert Tilton. I was miserable.

It really seemed to me that faith was something that I needed to work up – to prove to God so that I could earn His pleasure. But that can't be right can it? That would mean that it's not about grace anymore. It's about what *I* do. But doesn't it say that God's not pleased if I don't have it?

Let me ask you this: who creates this faith?

I've come to the understanding that faith has never been ours to begin with. The Apostle Paul understood faith as being a gift from God. In Romans 12:3, he says that God deals – or imparts – faith to us. It's His faith. Paul further elaborates on this thought when he talks about the Fruit of the Spirit. One of the Fruit being – you guessed it – faith. When the Holy Spirit is active in a person, when we remain in Him, the result is going to be faith.

Now tie it all together, and what we find is a beautiful relational dynamic of intimacy and dependency on God. We know God more, we experience His love, and we can trust Him. Faith is produced not by us – we're branches - but by Him when we remain vitally connected to Him.

When is God not pleased? When we don't have *real* faith. More specifically: When we're trying to work up faith on our own, when we deny grace, when we're trying to earn His love, when we're trying to con God into giving us something that He already wants us to give us (vow of faith), when we want to catch ourselves because we don't think He's good, when we try to produce independently of Him – these are all indicators of separation from God, brokenness, lack of knowing Him, the absence of His love, and it's not pleasing to Him.

God is pleased when we seek Him in those places where His love has not been revealed to us. God is pleased when we're authentic enough to say: "God I just don't trust You with this thing, but I want to." God is pleased when we declare that we're afraid or hopeless, and He gets to come save the day. That's what He does best – He's a Lover, a Fighter, a Savior. You're letting Him be who He is rather than trying to prove something.

71

THE BEAUTY OF CRISIS

It sure seems like faith would be a lot more appealing if it could be produced by God in really comfortable circumstances. Some of us would like to think that if everything was going perfectly that we'd know God more and we'd see His beauty and love.

My personal story of multiple tragedies and being bent, pulled, and contorted will be for another book. What I can tell you from watching a respiratory monitor while sitting at my wife's bedside in the hospital as she gasped for life for 72 hours straight is that sometimes we have to come grips with our smallness in order to know His Greatness. It goes against everything we know in culture to say "I'm weak. I'm needy." Sometimes it even goes against our Christian culture to say, "Help me with my unbelief." But it's the truth.

I don't think that God creates difficult circumstances. I don't think He creates tragedy. I think He grieves when we're hurt.

But God will seize the opportunity for us to know Him more. He'll go to the depths of our personal hell shielding us from the flames, proving He is still good, that He loves us, and that His power will enable us to overcome. And He produces a hope in us that defies logic, that even mocks the threat of our present circumstance.

I don't want life to get simpler. I want to rely on God. I'm not sure that I would believe in God if life was just carefree. I feel for people who've never had to go to dark places, or who have caught themselves and tried to make a way for themselves. They have missed God's best. They've missed getting to know Him.

I want to keep pursuing God to know Him, to be continually surprised at how He's going to respond in the most dire circumstances, to allow Him the opportunity to respond in an amazing way.

I seem to know what I'm talking about at times in this book, but I'm only now starting to see how God is so worth even difficulty. He's what I get at the end – the knowledge of Him as I experience His breakthrough, His power, and the creativity in how He answers all things.

All I can say is: Let Him love you. Know Him. Respond. Depend. Let His overcoming power bring peace, trust, and strength.

YOU EITHER BELIEVE IN GRACE OR YOU DON'T

Let's take it one step further though.

A couple of months back, I was asked, "I realize that we're not supposed to try to 'work up' things, but what about loving and having passion for God. Is that something we do on our own?"

That's a great question. And here's what I believe. I believe that even love, particularly the kind of perfect love that God is worthy of, is not something we're even capable of working up. It is a divine love. We are unable to love with all our hearts without the power of God.

It's perfectly alright to ask God to give us a passion for Him. We should ask Him to enable us to love Him more. It's not something we can do on our own. We're dependent people.

Grace is either everything or it's nothing. Grace is suffi-cient or we are self-suffient. If it ever falls short, if there is an ounce that we have to contribute on our own, then I think we should all question whether or not what Jesus did could really save us.

The bottom line is that we either believe in grace or we don't. If there is any place in our life – doing good things for God, overcoming sin, changing, having faith, - anything that is human effort, if we are the source of power, we deny grace, we separate ourselves from the power and love of Christ, and we wither.

Acts 17:28

...in Him we live, and move, and have our being.

COMMITMENT TIME

If you've ever been to church, a camp, or a retreat, you may have had your own experience with the infamous "commitment time." Maybe you've heard these words before: "I'm going to ask you to make a commitment..." Being an insider to the whole church service planning process, I'll tell you that this is what everything drives toward – a commitment by you. The assumption is that you'll make a commitment and, when you get back home, you'll change.

For me those were always intense, scary moments. Normally, it takes a while for people to respond, especially if it's some kind of altar call. A few people start trickling down to the front followed by more and more. Eventually – if the speaker is a guy who really brings it home – the seats will be emptied and everyone will be up front making a commitment.

Maybe you felt pressured, obligated, or coerced to join in. Or it's possible that you were encouraged by the fact that other people seemed to be able to make a commitment, and it strengthened you to be able to do it.

Regardless, it's scary. You're going up front. You have no idea what's going to happen up there. But you're even more unsure of what's going to happen when you walk away. After all, you've known your track record, your weaknesses, your shortcomings. You even know what happened the last time you made one of those commitments.

I think if we're honest, we're most terrified in those moments because we're making a commitment to God. After all, God's huge. He's perfect. He knows everything. And we just don't feel like we measure up to Him at all.

In the Old Testament, it was customary for commitments between people to be followed by a bloody ritual. We understand commitment to be described as covenant. When two people would make a covenant, stipulations as to the requirements of each person are laid out as well as penalties if the commitment isn't followed through. If the stipulations are met, then blessings and harmony would follow; however, if one fails, the end will be judgment.

Following everything that is spelled out, a ceremony takes place where an animal is cut in two, separated from head to tail. The two walk through symbolically sealing the commitment. With the bloody pieces of the animal on either side of them, they are each saying "May what has happened to these animals, happen to me if I break this covenant with you."

I found in Scripture a great example of this. In Genesis 15, God told Abram to go out and bring back some small livestock. Later on, Abram brings these things back to God and cuts each of them right down the middle. He takes the two pieces of cow and puts them across from one another. He does the same thing with a goat and a ram. It's difficult to picture an animal being cut in half, but it must have been a tedious process. Even if it had been a perfect, precision slice, there would have been blood everywhere. But when he was unprepared for the moment, he had to use whatever he could find. So I can imagine that by the time he put pressure out the animal's body and forcefully cut through its flesh, fat, muscle, and bone that blood was gushing out everywhere. After 3 animals, Abram is physically exhausted. But it's time to go through the ceremony of covenant. It's time to seal this thing. It's *commitment* time.

And then God does something really odd right at this defining moment. He causes Abram to fall into a deep sleep. In

Abram's state of utter weakness when he's physically unable to go on anymore, God awakens him just enough to spell out who *He* was, the stipulations for the commitment, as well as the details of the promises. Through tired eyes, Abram watches as God Himself walks through the blood and guts of the animals that were sacrificed.

And Abram is startled. Maybe he even rises to his feet and respectfully says: "Hey God, wait a minute. I've seen this ceremony before. I know how this works. I'm supposed to be walking through that with You, right?"

Wrong.

Abram couldn't have passed through and made a commitment like that to God. God was far too superior. And even if Abram had made a commitment to God as a servant would in those days, he could have never lived up to the stipulations.

So what God did has mind-blowing implications. God was saying, "'May what has happened to these animals, be done to *Me* if you break this commitment with Me." And you don't have to be a theologian to know how this commitment played out. It literally was done to Christ what was done to those animals. He was broken. He was sacrificed. God knew it all the way back then. That's why God made a commitment that could only be fulfilled by Himself.

I think Abram was overwhelmed. I think he understood: "God knows I can't make this commitment to Him, but He still wants to make it to me. He still wants to have a relationship with me. He wants to be bound to me despite my failure, even at His own expense."

Abram experienced grace. He knew it wasn't cheap, but it wasn't costing *him* anything.

What does all that mean? I think it means that God is asking us to make a commitment even today.

But it's not what you think.

We know those non-committal types don't we? Maybe we are one of them. People don't commit to things when there is a large degree of failure. Often people don't commit to people they really care about because they can't deal with the pain they'll cause if they break the commitment.

Commitment brings with it this sense of straining and effort doesn't it? Just saying it makes us uncomfortable.

Here's the thing though: strain and effort are feeble human attempts that are independent of God. Committing more or re-committing is anti-grace.

God does tell us to commit. He asks us to commit our ways to Him, to commit our lives to Him, to commit our hearts to Him. But this kind of commitment is different from human effort.

Psalm 37:5

Commit everything you do to the LORD. Trust Him, and He will do it.

When God asks us to commit, He is asking us to submit, hand over cleanly, depend, give away, trust in total reliance on Him to walk through everything for us.

Commitment isn't our increasing what we do, it is as John said, letting God be more for us and in our lives.

We must decrease.

God must increase.

08

heart response

ISN'T THAT WHAT YOU *DO?*

I'VE had the opportunity to work for some great churches over the years. All of my ministry experience has been in what has come to be known as the megachurch. It's often been jaw-dropping, as I've had the first hand experience of God doing some amazing things.

When I tell people what I do for a living, most think that it's super spiritual. After all, I go to work at a church. Isn't that God's house? I spend most of my day reading the Bible and praying. I wash my hands with holy water and have communion for breakfast – only one cracker though because I fast all throughout the workday. Of course, it's not really work. It's not like a job in the real world where you have to produce, hit sales numbers, set goals, and get home after 7pm.

If I keep going, you're just going to assume that I'm being being sarcastic.

The reality of ministry is that it all too often became a job. It didn't start out that way though. When you begin it's all about God, and this insatiable desire to see Him change the lives of people. Finally, something that you do clicks. It works so well that you assume that God is blessing the program. Sooner or later, and not in one fell swoop, you start serving the program more than you are the people you are trying to reach. More tragically, you serve the program more than God.

Often our conversations on staff turned more toward how many butts were in the seats, and "How can we do this better?" Rather than, "What do you think God is doing? Where is He leading us?" I'm ashamed to say that weeks, even months at a time, I was almost completely prayerless. "Isn't that what you *do*?" Well, it's supposed to be what ministers and pastors do, but I was too busy doing good things for God. I couldn't take the time to stop what I was doing.

Unfortunately, I'm not alone in feeling like that. Like me, most pastors and ministers I know are Type A, highly motivated, and task-oriented. Much is being produced, but our conversations on a more personal level reveal other things when they use these words to describe themselves: over-worked, dissatisfied, frustrated, empty, lonely, burnt out, stale with God, obsessed with comparison, hardhearted, uncompassionate. Marriages were often in disarray.

Kinda scary isn't it? But by all the standards, we are succeeding with honors.

These experiences brought to mind the letter that Jesus wrote to the church at Ephesus:

Revelation 2:2-5

I know your deeds, your hard work and your perseverance. You have persevered and have endured hardships for my name, and have not grown weary. Yet I hold this against you: You have forsaken your first love. Remember the height from which you have fallen! Repent and do the things you did at first.

Just like this early church, we were such a doing people. And let's face it, there is much to be done. There is a mission to be accomplished. The mission is to spread this news of Jesus to each and every person on the planet to bring them back into a relationship with God. Jesus said there was a great harvest – an enormous opportunity to reach out to people who want and need this - but very few workers. But He wants us to know that He's more concerned with our passionate pursuit of Him personally. The mission will come. We cannot confuse pursuing the mission with pursuing God. When we come to a place of emptiness, frustration, and exhaustion, it's a sure sign that something is wrong.

The place that Jesus wanted to bring these people back to was again focusing on love. And there's a really good reason for that: the mission is the byproduct of a regular, personal encounter with God.

This whole mission that God asks of us isn't a work of obligation. It's an act of relationship, and its purpose is love, because it is out of love that God allows us to be a part of what He is doing.

John 15:15

I no longer call you servants, because a servant does not know his master's business. Instead, I have called you friends, for everything that I learned from my Father I have made known to you.

God's mission flows out of love.

I think a lot of the guys I know in ministry who are ultra-successful by the world's standard are driven, but it's not flowing out of love from God. I think their basic need for love has not been met, and, to compensate, they have occupied themselves with goal setting and impossible standards in an effort to earn the love that they haven't experienced.

In *So I Send You*, Oswald Chambers wrote, "Any work for God that has less than a passion for Jesus Christ as its motive will end in crushing heartbreak and discouragement." And I would add that mission that is not firmly rooted and grounded in the love received from God will collapse and its personal destruction can even be catastrophic.

If you're still reading or possibly skipping ahead because this sounds like an earlier chapter of the book and I'm being redundant, then maybe you're still not getting it. We can't understand mission apart from love. We have no power; we have nothing to offer unless there is love first. When we dwell in Him, the mission – the vision, the passion, the ability, the power, the success, the place – will all flow naturally out of it.

Mission, doing anything good for God, and what Jesus was driving at in Revelation 2 can be summed up in one word: Response. Our heart has a response to the love that has been received from God. In the overflow of our heart, something happens. You know what that is?

We love. It's the natural response to unconditional love. We love God back. All that He desires, it happens. And out of a love response, comes the other stuff.

RELATIONAL MISSION

When I was kid, I really looked up to my brother, Kelly. In a time when Tom Selleck was considered a sex symbol, my brother was the envy of all his peers as he sported a full mustache at age 12. Looking back, I don't know what's more strange – my brother having a mustache at an unusual age or Tom Selleck being a sex symbol. Nevertheless, Kelly convinced me that all the girls were in to him, and he proved it to me by making out in front of me with his girlfriend in the church van on the way back from a trip to a semi-pro baseball game. I wanted to be just like him!

In the summer, my brother cut our neighbors' grass for extra money. I remember the distinctive sound the plastic flap would make as it dragged on the concrete as my brother pushed it down the sidewalk en route to the houses of his customers' blocks away. A farmer's tan later, he'd return with sweat in the crease of his neck holding onto bits of grass and mud. When he got around to it, he would cut our grass. It was a magnificent sight to behold watching him cut perfect geometric shapes into our lawn until it was a small square. I'd chase him in the trails that he made, and ultimately convince him to let me have a turn.

I was a very short kid so my arms could only comfortably grasp the bar that functioned as a brace on the mower. Not only did I have physics and structural design against me, I was weak, so I couldn't really do much with the mower. My brother would walk behind me with his hands on the main bar. I'd try to swat him away so that I could do it, and somehow he'd convince me that he was just keeping the mower straight within the lines as I couldn't see over the bar. I really didn't care about keeping it straight. I just wanted to push it, feel the beads of sweat on my forehead, and then quit whenever I got bored. I was a pretty annoying kid, but, for some strange reason, Kelly enjoyed sharing his work with me, even though I really wasn't a whole lot of help, and might have even been more of a setback.

I find some similarities in our mission with Jesus. It's *His* mission, by the way. *He* started it. *He* continues it. And *He's* going to be the one to complete it.

Us? We join Him in what He's doing. We don't have the strength at all to do it on our own. As a matter of fact, we sometimes swat away and try to take credit for what's happening, when all along Jesus has His hands on the bar making it go. Of course, we're doing even less than what we think we're doing because there's this whole Kingdom of God that's advancing and the power of the Holy Spirit. Otherwise, we'd just be pushing mowers.

We're not really needed, but it just seems like God refuses to do this without us. He gets a special joy out of working through our weakness. The problem for us though is that, for the most part of our lives, we've struggled to admit our weakness. Dependence doesn't seem that appealing to us.

Regardless, dependence is essential, and it was something that Jesus modeled when it came to work of the Father. Love and dependence was the foundation of His ministry. He never sought to establish His worth any other way. No one tricked Him, badgered Him, or guilted Him into doing anything that He wasn't supposed to do. Not that they didn't try. At times He healed, other times He didn't, and more times than not, when it seemed He could benefit the most, He did the opposite.

Jesus described this relational ministry for us, and it helps us understand how we relate to God in the work that He's called us to do:

John 5:16-19

Jesus said to them, "My Father is always at His work to this very day, and I, too, am working." For this reason the Jews tried all the harder to kill Him; not only was He breaking the Sabbath, but He was even calling God His own Father, making Himself equal with God. Jesus gave them this answer: "I tell you the truth, the Son can do nothing by Himself; He can do only what He sees His Father doing, because whatever the Father does the Son also does.

Would you have said that Jesus' life was normal? You might be thinking, "No, it's not normal." It really depends on *who's* saying normal. Because in Jesus life and times, what He did on a daily basis drawing crowds to Himself of the people who just wanted to hear Him speak, blessing kids, feeding thousands of people with a kid's meal from Long John Silver's was normal. People walked who'd never walked. People gained hearing who'd never heard. People saw the sunrise who'd never seen the light of day. People dead and in their graves - rigormortis had settled in; they were stinking and somehow their lungs expanded and the blood flowed through their veins again - this was all a day in the life of Christ. It was normal.

We struggle with the fact that Scripture says, "We'll do those same things, even greater things." We discount it. We say, "Jesus didn't really mean that." Or we just dis-qualify ourselves as people who don't have enough faith or something.

The question I'd pose is: "Why doesn't our life read more like that?" When we discount or invalidate what Jesus Himself spoke, I think it's just a copout. I think it's be-cause we struggle with the fact that there are stories that have yet to be written in our lives

Now, we're not going back to a "work it up, "Let me try to make something happen," mentality. What we are going to do instead is respond to our hearts; because in our hearts, there is a voice that's saying that there has to be more. There's got to be more that what you're living.

RELATIONAL RESPONSE

How did Jesus live out this life? If you notice, no place was
safe when He was walking the planet. He did a few things
in church (the synagogue), but the whole of His ministry
was spent among real people, among the broken, in a broken world. Things broke out when Jesus was walking into
cities, attending weddings, fishing - even when he was 3
days late for funerals. And the reason wasn't just because
He was God in the flesh. Jesus modeled a way of relating
to God as He did ministry.

Jesus remained intimately connected to God the Father.
He got away if that's what He needed to do. But the important thing is that when He left those times of solitude, He
didn't walk away from the Father. He remained with Him.

Countless times, Jesus urged us to remain with Him. It's
not that we're ever on our own, but aren't there times when
we seem more aware of God than others? I find that there
have been times when God seemed more present than normal. But that's not because He actually was, it just meant
that I was more sensitive to Him. We have to learn to remain in Him, even as we go out to do the stuff in the
ordinary, every day.

As Jesus moved along in His day, needs would seem to find
Him. Now granted, some people would just drag their fami-
lies and friends to Jesus, but that wasn't always the case.
Jesus, remaining in the Father, saw the need and knew
how God desired to respond. And when He felt the heart-
beat of the Father, He joined in on what the Father was
doing.

I have a habit that some people might find strange. Actually, it's probably more of a discipline, but I pray with eyes
wide open. I know, I know, that breaks some kind of religious rule or something. I remember having my eyes open
during a prayer when I was in a kindergarten Sunday
School class. At the end of class, our teacher told me to

stick around after everyone had left. She pulled me aside and told me "Jesus was very sad that you had your eyes open during prayer." I was busted. "How did she know?" I remember thinking.

Why do we close our eyes? We close our eyes for our benefit. We close our eyes so we aren't embarrassed or distracted by other people who are around. We close our eyes to block out distractions and have a personal moment. Those are the reasons.

But I've found that I close my eyes mostly when I'm asleep. I learned a while back that a third of our life is spent sleeping – we're literally unconscious through one-third of our lives! And another 20 – 25% is spent waiting, preparing, taking showers, and using the bathroom. More than half of our life is in complete stagnation.

So when it comes to prayer, I don't want to shut the world out. I want to be fully conscious and aware of what God is doing. Often I'll pray just short breath prayers even when I'm walking around Wal-mart: "God, show me what you're doing around me. Show me where You're working, so I can join You and be a part of it." I keep my eyes open with expectation, and God does respond. Sometimes He just speaks to me. Sometimes there's a small way in which I help someone. Just yesterday, out of nowhere, I had a conversation with a barista at Starbucks about deep spiritual matters. The guy didn't even know me, and he started spilling his guts in front of everyone. And it happened simply out of just keeping my eyes open and being willing to be inconvenienced when God was ready to do something.

LOVE TO OTHERS

Mark 12:30-31

Love the Lord your God with all your heart and with all your soul and with all your mind and with all your strength.' The second is this: 'Love your neighbor as yourself.' There is no commandment greater than these."

I think we forget a lot that we're supposed to love people. The fact that we're supposed to love people like we love ourselves, and some other really difficult things like loving our enemies, seem like impossible tasks.

And there's good reason for feeling like it's impossible. Do you know why? Because it is. It's not humanly possible to love people sacrificially and by choice regardless if they hate us.

Love for people, just like everything in the mission, is based on response. We can only love people as much as we have truly experienced the love of God. That's why you see Scriptures that tell us to forgive as Christ forgave us, love your wife like Christ loved the Church. Our depth of knowledge and experience is what enables us to respond. I think people who have a difficult time forgiving, have never experienced forgiveness. I think people who are selfish, greedy graspers, who aren't lovingly generous have not experienced the generosity of God. People who are reckless tyrants don't know and haven't experienced the patience and unconditional love of God.

The mission is fueled by love from God for us. It changes us, and the overflow of that love is redirected toward the world.

LOVE THAT CHANGES THE WORLD

We all know that we're supposed to care. We know we *should* love people. I think maybe we underestimate love. We don't realize how it could change the world, or how a fuller expression of it could change us.

Do you think you *know* God? Do you think you *know* His love?

For years, I ran past this verse as I read through the book of Matthew. It never jumped out to me because I hadn't really experienced God's love for me, nor knew how that could impact me to change the world.

Matthew 9:36

"Seeing the people, [Jesus] felt compassion for them."

In the book, *Organic Church*, Neil Cole brought this verse to life:

"...The busier I get, the less I care about others. When Jesus saw the crowds, He saw more than an obstacle getting in the way of His mission. He saw His mission, and He felt compassion for them. For Jesus however, His body reacted to His compassion. It was an immediate and physical response. He felt it. Actually, in the original language this is one word: *splancthna*. The word for compassion is quite descriptive; it literally means "bowels."

There is good reason for using this descriptive word. When you feel really emotional, where do you feel it? The first time we men picked up the phone to call a special girl and ask her out, we felt it in our *splanc-thna*. When the doctor has crushing news from the results of your blood test or biopsy, you feel it first in your *splancthna*.

So when Jesus saw all the people, His breath was taken away. He was hit in the solar plexus. He was bent over in discomfort.

The Bible reveals why He felt compassion for them. It is because He saw them as distressed and downcast, like sheep without a shepherd. The two words translated "distressed" and "downcast" are also highly descriptive. They are violent words. Dis-

tressed can be translated as "harassed," or even as
molested." The word downcast is a wrestling term
that can be translated as "pinned down by force."

If we really saw people like this, there's no doubt we'd be
motivated. We're so hesitant. We're so, frankly, uncaring
that we don't get involved. We're afraid; we're too busy; we
don't want to be inconvenienced; or we don't want to in-
volve ourselves in personal matters.

If there was a child across your street that you knew was
being molested, you would get involved. Fear, being late for
work, being inconvenienced, getting too personally involved
would not be a concern of yours. 90 year old grannies
would march across the street with a walker and kick the
front door down to save the child.

What kind of Jesus followers would we be, what kind of impact, how world changing would it be if became people who
felt the expression of love that Jesus has for each person on
the planet. Do you think that could make a difference? I
do.

I know I want to love like that. I have to admit I'm not
there yet. But I'm asking God to work that in me. It's not
possible up to me, but by His grace and the power of His
Spirit, it can happen.

And it *can* happen for you as well, when you experience His
love, when you get to know Him, when you quit trying to
force it and lean in to His grace and rely on His power.

What does God want from you?

He just wants your heart. Are you willing to give it to Him?

09

epilogue

THE most difficult thing about writing a book to me is clarity. I wanted to be concise, but sometimes I wondered if I said enough or left something out that was really important. I didn't start out with the intention of even writing an epilogue because, well, who reads those things anyway? But I felt it necessary for my own conscience to pull it together in an unfragmented sort of way as I intended it to come out.

My daughter, Jadyn brings a smile to my face every time she tells someone Jesus lives in her heart. I remember being quizzed as a child: "Where does Jesus live?" The correct response was "In my heart!" I think that's still a pretty accurate picture of redemption and sanctification, and that's what I've tried to unpack here.

The first essential is that we would experience love in our hearts. God sent His Son, and Jesus came into our hearts because we believed that God loved us. I don't believe that the average Christian has really experienced that. It hasn't formed us because we're not rooted and grounded in it. God really bet the house on love though. If we just knew and experienced the depths of God's love, we'd truly forever be changed. And we would change the world out of a response to that love.

At His baptism, Jesus heard the words "I love You. I am pleased with you." I figure if Jesus needed to hear them, they're pretty important for us as well. These words marked the beginning of Jesus' public ministry. He'd never done anything for God up to that point - at least nothing notable enough to be included in the Bible. 33 years of what? Intimacy. And it was out of the affirming voice of God – God's embrace – that Jesus received a profound awareness of the Father's affectionate love.

Jesus referred to His Father's love for Him many times. "The Father loves the Son," He would say. He connected that love with what He had to do. Because the Father loves Him, the Father lets Him be a part of what He's doing.

Jesus wanted us to be assured of that love as well; as a matter of fact, it's one of the primary jobs of the Holy Spirit in us. Romans 5:5 says that the Holy Spirit pours the love of God in our hearts and cries in us "Abba, Father," and bears witness in our spirits that we are God's children (Romans 8:15-16; Galatians 4:6).

Long before the Lord's Prayer became that robotic, heart-numbing, absent-minded background noise of Sunday mornings, it was a passionate, controversial prayer that Jesus taught His followers. Narrowly escaping being stoned to death in John 10 over calling God *His* "Father," Jesus perplexes and infuriates the religious when He tells His disciples to do the same thing.

The word He used for Father was "Abba" – an informal, intimate way to express a tender, affectionate love. It expressed trust, belonging, and intimacy. He said, "God wants you to call Him 'Daddy.' He wants to move you towards that place with Him where it's not just a mere word but a natural expression of your heart."

I'm sure that shook everyone up, because up to that point, the Jews had been referring to God in a very impersonal way.

You know, the name that you call a person says a lot about your relationship with them.

What do you call teachers at school...Mr. or Mrs. Or Ms.
What do you call your boss...Mr. or Mrs. – usually not with their first names.
What do you call a pastor...Reverend or Brother, etc.
What do you call your best friend...usually by their first name

Often we have nicknames for people. Those can be good or bad. Many times though, nicknames say something deeper about a relationship. Most people who know me know that I call my wife, "Mochacita." That nickname has stuck ever since our honeymoon in Cancun. She got this really dark tan and looked like an island girl. I took 8 levels of Spanish which has enabled me to have the conversational ability of an 18 month old child. There were a few things that I did pick up, and I told Jessica that the interpretation of Mochacita was "little brown girl." A few years ago, Jessica said, "You never call me by my first name anymore, how come?" I said, "You know, you're right." And without really having to think about it, I said, "You know, calling you Mochacita is much more intimate to me than calling you by your first name."

You see, I call her by a name that expresses my personal experience with her. If anybody else calls her, "Mochacita" – it's pretty stupid. You know why? Because they don't *know* her by that name. It has happened though. A friend of ours once called Jessica that and she and I looked at each other like, "What the...who does *he* think he is calling you that?"

It blows me away that God could have rightfully required us to call Him something grandiose and abstract. But instead, God chooses for us to call Him "Daddy." And If God wants us to call Him "Daddy," it means He wants us to experience Him that way.

Not only does He want us to know Him by that name, but He wants us to get our identity from His name. We really are His sons and daughters. And if we see ourselves that way, we will approach Him much differently.

When we go hang out with people, we usually prepare for those times by showering, dressing up, using breathmints, and watching the clock so we're on time.
If it's our parents, we wouldn't think of preparing for those moments. We may or may not brush our teeth or hair. We walk into the house without knocking. We rummage in the refrigerator like we own the place. We pick up the phone whether they're on it or not. We wouldn't care. Because we know we have that access. And we probably wouldn't get in trouble for it either.

With God, it's exactly the same way - We have access to Him 24/7 and He actually longs and waits for the times when we'll show up spontaneously unannounced simply because we desire to be with Him.

Hebrews 4:16

Let us then approach the throne of grace with confidence, so that we may receive mercy and find grace to help us in our time of need.

Imagine what it would be like if we knew God so well that we called Him Daddy. If we knew ourselves so well that we knew we were so favored that we could rummage around in the refrigerator of God's Kingdom - not like beggars, but - like we own it. We'd no longer jump through hoops, nor would we try to clean ourselves up before going there. We'd confidently say, "Here I am. Don't you *love* me?"

And you know what God would do? He'd hop off His throne in an instant to scoop us up!

How differently would we live life?

Sometimes I look at things like loving enemies and the simple fact that Jesus went to death being obedient. I used to wonder how He could do something like that? Mortals in stature weren't as big as ants in comparison.

I look at my own life and how I'll fight to win an argument, or to one-up someone, or to save face. It's an absolute pathetic display – like two kids fighting over a mudpie. We're so convinced that there is worth in titles and stuff on this planet, when the truth is, if it can die with you or be taken away, it's worthless.

How could He have possibly given up the right to be called and worshiped as God and submit Himself over to be brutally embarrassed, beaten, and stripped naked by evil men?

Because His worth and identity weren't given or bound by earth, titles, or His own works. It couldn't be taken away. His understanding of who He was and His favor with God was the foundation of His identity. He never sought to establish His worth any other way.

We struggle with humility because we don't even get who we are and what we already possess. People only strive and fight for things that they have either lost or fear losing. In Christ, we truly have everything.

The other day, my friend Ammar said, "'God loves you' is the foundation of everything. It's so basic. But it's still a concept that's impossible to grasp by just telling someone it's true."

I agreed. That's why I didn't spend my time in this book trying to prove God's love by giving definitions of it. It is all over Scripture, and Jesus' sacrifice speaks it the loudest. But I mostly didn't include all of those things, because it is truly a relational dynamic. You simply can't be told that love. It must be experienced.

I recall being in the delivery room for the birth of our youngest, Jadyn. We knew we were parents about 6 weeks in. We had give-us-baby-stuff parties, went to the classes, brought our oldest Victoria to sibling classes, picked out a name, saw the baby in multiple ultrasounds; we even talked to the baby most days. But nothing could have prepared me for that moment of birth. I was stunned: "Whoa, there was a baby in there this whole time!" It was long before then a reality, but only in that moment did reality finally become tangible for me.

And I could have never prepared for the flood of emotion that felt like a heavy 50 foot wave crashing over me. All I knew was love. I could barely recognize this purple slimy being as mine. She'd never spoken a word. She'd never accomplished anything. She had nothing to offer me. As a matter of fact, she was pretty indifferent to me. But I would have given my life for her. I couldn't believe I could possibly love someone like that. I was simply undone – lost in love. I couldn't even gasp for breath for fear of drowning.

And in that moment, I sensed the presence of God. And Daddy said, "Now you've experienced an ounce of depth of love I have for you."

I've had times when you could barely recognize me as His. I've never accomplished anything truly great. I have nothing to offer Him. I've spent most of my life indifferent to Him. But just for a shot at having me. He gave His life for me. And I can't believe He loves me like that. I'm undone – lost in this love. I can't breathe for fear of drowning.

There are still times where I go back to performing. There are times when I look in the mirror and I'm confronted with the things that make me not worthy of being loved. There are still times when I strive and want to prove my worth. There are still times of meltdown.

And whenever that happens, whenever the dysfunction ensues, I'm pointed back to my loss of relationship. My missing Love.

God's ready to leave a mark on your heart. There's a buzz in the air right now. Do you feel it? It's God putting the needles into the inkwells of love. If you'd just lay bare your heart, He can make it right, He can heal it, and He can forever tattoo you with His love.

**INTERACT WITH PAUL
& OTHER READERS AT:**

www.TATTOOontheHEART.com

BIBLIOGRAPHY

Chapter 1

Theological Dictionary of the Old Testament, Volume III. (1974) G. Johannes Botterweck, Helmer Ringgren, Heinz-Josef Fabry. Pg. 16-17

Matthew 22;34-40; Mark 12:28-34

Ephesians 3:17-19

Luke 8:4-10

Chapter 3

Victory Over the Darkness. Neil Anderson. 2000

Chapter 4

In this chapter I talk a great deal about the resolve of the heart as well as how God desires to have it. Some pastors might disagree. I've known some who like to point out the Scripture in Jeremiah 17:9 that speaks of the heart being "deceitful and wicked." I adhere to the promise of God that he was going to give us a new, undivided heart. A wicked heart is one that has not been saved and transformed by God.

Our hearts, like the whole of our beings, are in the process of sanctification. The Holy Spirit is constantly at work making us more like Jesus.

I'd also add that I grew up in a religious tradition that wasn't very big on emotions or any part of our being that wasn't our soul(spirit). Their oversensitivity brings to mind the Gnostics who were religious heretics in the New Testament. Essentially there were two groups of Gnostics. One group felt like since the soul had been saved, it didn't really matter what you did in the body. The other group believed that the soul was good, but the body was bad, so they rejected anything that was not soul.

Jesus didn't come into your life for you to be a robot with no emotion. The passions were created by God. Our drives are good, but tainted. We can't be ruled by emotions, but we're not fully alive without them. Jesus came to save our total beings, not just souls. Just a reminder that when we are in a final perfected state that we will be a total being with a physical body, a heart & mind, and our soul/spirit.

Physical Life - Acts 14:17; Jas. 5:5;
Moral nature and spiritual life, grief, John 14:1; Rom. 9:2; 2 Cor. 2:4;
Joy, John 16:22; Eph. 5:19;
The desires, Matt. 5:28; 2 Pet. 2:14;
The affections, Luke 24:32; Acts 21:13;
The perceptions, John 12:40; Eph. 4:18;
The thoughts, Matt. 9:4; Heb. 4:12;
The understanding, Matt. 13:15; Rom. 1:21;
The reasoning powers, Mark 2:6; Luke 24:38;
The imagination, Luke 1:51;
The conscience, Acts 2:37; 1 John 3:20;
The intentions, Heb. 4:12, cp. 1 Pet. 4:1;
Purpose, Acts 11:23; 2 Cor. 9:7;
The will, Rom. 6:17; Col. 3:15;
Faith, Mark 11:23; Rom. 10:10; Heb. 3:12.

Deuteronomy 6:5

Isaiah 29:13

Jeremiah 24:7

1 Samuel 16:7

The New Thayer's Greek-English Lexicon of the NT, Joseph Henry Thayer, Hendrickson, Peabosy, Ma, 1981, p. 3

Wuest's Word Studies, From the Greek New Testament, Vol 3, Eerdmans Publishing Co, Grand Rapids, Mi, 1992, #28, p. 62

Chapter 5

Matthew 11:29

2 Corinthians 3:12-18

John 14:26; John 15:26; Romans 8:16

Thayer's and Smith's Bible Dictionary Greek Lexicon

Romans 11:33; Ephesians 3:8

Chapter 6

Barna Group Ltd. *Barna Update* September 8, 2004

Real Teens: A Contemporary Snapshot of Youth Culture.
George Barna. 2001

Chapter 7

Galatians 4:8-11

Chapter 8

Oswald Chambers, *So Send I You* (Bristol, U.K.: Marshall
Morgan & Scott, 1988)

Neil Cole, Organic Church (San Francisco: Jossey-Bass
2005) pg.145-147

Send your comments to:

comments@tattooontheheart.com

**INTERACT WITH PAUL
& OTHER READERS AT:**

www.TATTOOontheHEART.com

Made in the USA
Charleston, SC
23 December 2013